I0820622

Overtones of Opera in American Literature from Whitman to Wharton

Overtones of Opera in American Literature from Whitman to Wharton

Carmen Trammell Skaggs

Louisiana State University Press
Baton Rouge

Published by Louisiana State University Press

Manufactured in the United States of America
FIRST PRINTING

DESIGNER: *Amanda McDonald Scallan*
TYPEFACES: *Text: Whitman; Display: Lucida Calligraphy*
PRINTER AND BINDER: *Thomson-Shore, Inc.*

Library of Congress Cataloging-in-Publication Data

Skaggs, Carmen Trammell, 1976–
Overtones of opera in American literature from Whitman to Wharton / Carmen Trammell Skaggs.
p. cm.
Includes bibliographical references and index.
ISBN 978-0-8071-3491-7 (cloth : alk. paper)
1. American literature—History and criticism. 2. Opera in literature. I. Title.
PS121.S545 2009
810.9'3578—dc22

2009013463

This publication was funded in part by a Columbus State Faculty Development Grant.

The paper in this book meets the guidelines for permanence and durability of the Committee on Production Guidelines for Book Longevity of the Council on Library Resources. ∞

To my son, Nathan,
who fills each day with creativity,
wonderment, and delight

Contents

Acknowledgments

I gratefully acknowledge *Mosaic: A Journal for the Interdisciplinary Study of Literature* for permission to reprint a version of "Looking through the Opera Glasses: Performance and Artifice in *The Age of Innocence*" in chapter four. The essay first appeared in *Mosaic* 37.1 (March 2004): 49–62.

For their wise suggestions during the drafting and revising of this project, I extend my gratitude to Kristin Boudreau, Hubert McAlexander, and Anne Williams.

With appreciation and admiration, I acknowledge my parents, Robert and Menlia Trammell, who introduced me to opera and literature, instilling a lifelong love of these arts.

Overtones of Opera in American Literature from Whitman to Wharton

Introduction

America and opera were born in the same year. In 1607, the year of Jamestown's establishment in the New World, Monteverdi's *Orfeo,* the first great opera, premiered in Mantua. Joseph Kerman describes the achievement in this way: "*Orfeo* is the first opera to reveal the characteristic composer's struggle with the libretto" (29). Musicologists consider the seventeenth-century composer the "founder of that tradition of opera-as-drama that passed through Gluck and Wagner, and, indeed, through most of the composers who have been accorded the highest prestige in histories of music" (Lindenberger, *Opera in History* 49). Many years passed, however, before opera came to America. The then-largest metropolitan cities—Boston, Charleston, New Orleans, New York, and Philadelphia—strove to be America's cultural centers. Charleston hosted America's first performance of a ballad opera, Colley Cibber's *Flora, or Hob in the Well,* in 1735, and *The Beggar's Opera* came to New York in 1750 (Dizikes 17–18). Historical records confirm the arrival of opera in New Orleans in 1796 and in Boston in 1797. These initial performances planted the seed for the flowering of opera in the New World.

From the late 1700s until the Civil War, New Orleans was the center of opera in America. Unlike other American cities producing opera, New Orleans boasted the only opera company—at times as many as three companies—to perform continuously, interrupted only by the Civil War (Kmen vii). In New Orleans, opera reflected the strong influence of French culture and language—favoring the works of French composers, importing artists from France, and performing operas in French. Rather than fearing the foreign element of opera, New Orleans embraced it. But New Orleans did not exclude other forms of opera. "It is true that the repertoire before the 1830s was primarily French and was what we now call light opera—but that was the opera of the time," Kmen comments. "As opera itself changed and developed, the opera in New Orleans kept pace. Thus when Caldwell

[James Caldwell] imported Italian companies in 1836 and 1837 the way had been prepared by the French company" (Kmen 199). While other American cities, under the influence of nationalism, rejected opera because they considered it alien and strange, New Orleans promoted it.

New Orleans played a pivotal role in the development and reception of this hybrid art form from the Southern gulf coast to the cities of the Eastern seaboard, influencing the operatic tastes of those who never visited Louisiana. With more than fifty artists on tour from 1827 to 1833, the Orleans Theater opera company under the direction of John Davis influenced the musical tastes of several other major metropolitan cities.

> Boston, Philadelphia, and Baltimore got their first tastes of a regular opera company; and in the two latter cities, the success of Davis' production of *Der Freischutz* presented a sharp contrast to the costly failure of local productions of the same opera shortly before. New York, to be sure, had already encountered grand opera when Manuel Garcia's company played in the two seasons immediately preceding the visits of the New Orleans company. But it found the latter [New Orleans company] to be "fully equal to that we imported from foreigners," and it enjoyed six seasons of such opera in what otherwise would have been a barren period. (Kmen 125)

Despite the New Orleans influence, however, New York served as the primary source of operatic experience for American writers.

The Beggar's Opera appeared at New York's Nassau Street Theater in 1750. Though not grand opera, the performance of this English ballad opera indicates the presence of and interest in the operatic form. But until New York's introduction to Italian opera, the city's theatergoers did not confront the questions of opera's intelligibility or the nationalist opposition to the form. In *As I Remember: Recollections of American Society during the Nineteenth Century*, Marian Gouverneur recalls: "The musical world of New York lay dormant until about the year 1825, when Dominick Lynch, much to the delight of the cultivated classes, introduced the Italian Opera. Through his instrumentality Madame Malibran, her father Signor Garcia, and her brother, Manuel

García [. . .] came to this country and remained for quite a period" (81). Dominick Lynch provided the financial backing for the Garcías' performances in New York, but two other men also negotiated the arrangements. As John Dizikes explains, "Lorenzo Da Ponte, Mozart's erstwhile librettist, now living in New York, used London friends to persuade García that he would make his fortune in the United States. Stephen Price, manager of the Park Theatre in New York and at one time manager of London's Drury Lane Theatre, worked out the performance arrangements" (4). Although the 1825 production introduced Italian opera to New York, it would be several years before a hall was built solely for opera. In the meantime, several other theaters in the city hosted operatic performances, including the New York Theater (the Bowery), Richmond Hill, Niblo's, and Castle Garden.[1]

About ten years after the Garcías' initial performance at the Park Theater, Da Ponte, at the age of eighty-five, insisted that the main hindrance to opera's flowering in New York was the lack of a proper opera house. "Italian opera presupposed an Italian opera house," Da Ponte believed. Determined to remedy the situation, Da Ponte gathered a group of subscribers who contributed $150,000 for the land and the building. New York's Italian Opera House opened for an initial season in November 1833 (Dizikes 75). After only two seasons, however, it closed because of its substantial debt, and it was sold in 1836. Despite the multitude of venues for performances, New York remained unwilling or unable to support a theater devoted primarily to opera until the opening of the Academy of Music in 1854. In between the building of Da Ponte's Italian Opera House and the opening of the Academy, two other opera houses were built in New York: Palmo's Opera House in 1844 and the Astor Place Opera House in 1847.[2] Although neither venue operated as an opera theater more than five years, they reflected an increasing level of interest in the art form as the city grew into an industrial and cultural center.[3]

New England's cultural center, Boston, promoted the literary arts, but lingering Calvinist and Puritan influence made it skeptical about theatrical arts. New England harbored "a cluster of attitudes hardened by history into conventional stereotypes: dislike of the theater, suspicion of art that was not useful, fear of art that emphasized feeling and unrestrained emotion" (Dizikes 149). As a result, music was promoted and performed for sacred or didactic purposes. Despite such prejudices, the city was introduced to opera by the staging of Grétry's *Richard the Lion Heart* in 1797. Like New Orleans and New York, Boston eventually decided that it, too, needed a venue just for opera. At the mayor's urging, Boston's businessmen undertook the building of a theater for opera in 1852. The mayor explained the necessity for the house: "Traveling businessmen, who might otherwise neglect to visit Boston would be attracted to the city by the dramatic and operatic entertainment such a theater could provide and would be likely to remain in the city longer for the same reason" (qtd. in Dizikes 165). Opening on September 11, 1854, the Boston Theatre presented Auber's *Les Diamants de la couronne* as its first opera. Although the building's beginnings were prompted by strictly mercenary concerns, the opera house provided a suitable setting for many cultural endeavors, including spoken drama. By the Civil War, opera had come to dominate the bill of the Boston Theatre, with traveling opera companies performing frequently.

The post–Civil War industrial boom led to the rise of new wealth in the commercial capitals of the nation. "In 1800 there had not been a single man with $1 million on Manhattan," Allen Churchill writes. "Forty years later the town boasted eight individuals worth more than $1 million; John Jacob Astor was supreme at $50 million. This necessitated the invention of the word 'millionaire,' which had not previously existed. There were also 840 other male citizens of the city worth $100,000 or more. This, in itself, was a fortune for the day" (Churchill 32). Looking for new ways to spend and display their wealth, these investors promoted art forms like opera. As Thorstein Veblen explains, "In order to gain and to hold the esteem of men it is not sufficient merely to possess wealth or power. The wealth or power must be put in evidence, for esteem is awarded only on evidence" (42).

Sensing instability in the ranks of New York's aristocracy, the new industrialist tycoons attempted to achieve a place in New York's social hierarchy by their patronage of the arts. Viewing art as a commodity and a key to status, the nouveaux riches recognized that opera presented an opportunity to consume and display their wealth. However, New York's only opera house in 1880 was the Academy of Music—a venue largely supported by the Knickerbockers—New York's most established families. As Churchill comments: "There the Knickerbocracy had contrived to maintain a last foothold, for the eighteen boxes at the Academy were passed from father to son by Old Guard families like Livingston, Cutting, Bayard, Duer, Beekman, Schermerhorn, Schuyler, and Barlow. Heading the affairs of the Academy were Pierre Lorillard, August Belmont, and Robert L. Cutting. Years before Mrs. Astor had succeeded in obtaining a box, but otherwise the Old Guard held firm" (134). According to Lloyd Morris, the Academy of Music played two distinct roles for the old aristocracy—display and diversion:

> Opera was essential to the fashionable, the socially elect. For where else but in the Academy's boxes—fortunately so limited in number—could you perform the obligatory rituals of public display? Was not society morally bound to show itself to the people in full regalia of ball dresses and jewels? Besides, opera was a social convenience. It filled the otherwise vacant hours before balls and late evening receptions. It enabled you to exchange brief intermission visits with your friends. It was an infallible register of social standing—you could measure the precise degree of your power, or the probable success of the debutante daughter whom you were anxiously launching, by the number of gentlemen who, during the intervals, entered your box to pay their respects. The boxes of the Academy were as competitive an institution as the Stock Exchange, as exciting in their prospects of dazzling fortune or ignominious failure—a costly parade ground for vanity and intrigue, courtship and heartbreak. (Morris 69)

In fact, opera provided one of the primary settings for the most visible contest between New York's oldest families and the newly minted millionaires of the industrial boom. When the families of New York's new wealth—the Vanderbilts, Roosevelts, Goulds, Morgans, and Whitneys—expressed interest in obtaining box seats at the Academy, they met ardent opposition. Refusing to be outdone, however, they created their own opera house when "fifty-two founders agreed to subscribe $10,000 each for boxes and in return received one hundred shares of stock valued at $100 a share. Thirteen more later joined as founders before the house's opening" (Cone 3). The new edifice, the Metropolitan Opera House, included 122 boxes and cost $1,732,478.71 to build.[4] The new opera house created a twofold rivalry—an artistic battle and a war of social privilege. Ultimately, the Metropolitan Opera House triumphed on both fronts.

> The Metropolitan Opera House, perhaps more than any other civic institution, embodied the values of the city's late nineteenth-century aristocracy. The greatest and most distinguished families in the city were present. These were men who controlled the banks and insurance companies, who dominated the boards of directors of the mining companies and railroads. Together, they made a great assertion of wealth, position, and apparent social solidarity. They shared a sense of possession: this was their world, around them were their relations, their opera house, their glittering gowns and jewels, and their mansions up and down Fifth Avenue. (Homberger 227)

Some historians see the rivalry between the Academy of Music and the Metropolitan Opera House as a showdown between the aristocracy and the plutocracy (Churchill 136), but the nouveau riche founders of the Met did not intend this conflict as the result. Instead, they hoped to establish themselves as the new American aristocracy. Dizikes notes that "the subscription system, in which boxes were bought for the season, to be used or not used as the subscriber wished, became the prevailing American system. This was a form of privilege, based on money, not social standing. It was the logical outcome of middle-class patronage—patronage by a plutocracy" (63). America's new wealthy did not envision opera as the medium for expressing democratic values. Instead, they wished to use it to establish wealth, not ancestry, as the measure of social status in New York.

Opera Moves from American Venues to American Verse

A few years after Walt Whitman's birth, Italian opera arrived in New York. On November 29, 1825, Rossini's *Il Barbiere di Siviglia*, performed at the Park Theatre, proved a sensation. While the press and the public recognized the significance of the event, some critics questioned opera's wide appeal to the American public—one that demanded drama with a "natural-born subject" that "represents the actions and passions of men as we see them in the world at large" ("The Opera" 239). The reviewer commented that, "from what we had previously read of it [the Italian opera], we always esteemed it a forced and unnatural bantling; seeing it has not changed our opinion" (239). Though Whitman initially expressed similar doubts about opera's ability to indicate a "perfect understanding of American realities" (*New York* 22), he defied the assumption that opera belonged to the European elite by translating opera into the poetry of democracy. Having searched the lowbrow entertainments of folk art in vain, Whitman found in the free form expression of bel canto opera a perfect model for his own experimentation with poetic form, creating a distinctly American voice.

Walt Whitman's introduction to opera coincides with its early development in New York. In his writings, Whitman recalls attending opera at the old Park, the Bowery, Broadway, and Chatham-square theatres, Chambers-street, Astor-place, the Battery, Castle Garden (Whitman, *Complete* 1: 24–27), and the Academy of Music (Traubel 3: 104). Working for journals, Whitman used a pressman's pass to attend the performances, and his first opera review appeared in the *Brooklyn Daily Eagle* on March 23, 1847 (Faner 7). In "Reminiscences of Walt Whitman," John Trowbridge recalls Whitman's observation that "but for the opera, I could never have written *Leaves of Grass*" (166). Influenced by the Romantic Transcendentalists, Whitman inherits and illustrates Emerson's concept of the poet as the only figure able to integrate the perceptions of eye, mind, and spirit. Through the poet's vision, a journey of transcendent exploration allows man to move seamlessly from a natural world into a spiritual realm. Whitman fuses the sights and sounds of nature with the sounds of music and man. He explains the embodying of poetic perception in one of his reviews: "You listen to this music, and the songs, and choruses—all of the highest range of composition known to the world of melody. A new world,—a liquid world—rushes like a torrent through you" (*New York* 22).

By emphasizing the physicality of the singer and the voice, Whitman also explores the erotic potential of an embodied art. Using the metaphor of opera, he celebrates American democracy, human sexuality, poetic creativity, and natural beauty. In *The Brown Decades: A Study of the Arts in America, 1865–1895,* Lewis Mumford explains that the doctrines of Emerson, Whitman, and Thoreau "brought a new confidence to all the other arts [besides literature]: Emerson's gospel of self-reliance and his belief in a fresh start, Whitman's hearty affirmation of the vulgarities and commonplaces of life, and Thoreau's deep sense of the landscape and its influences—all these beliefs were to have their effect upon the painter and the architect and the engineer" (26). Just as the doctrines of early American writers influenced the development of art in America, opera, a transplanted art form, influenced American writers like Whitman. Ironically, this highbrow art form provided the model of poetic expression for the celebrator of the commonplace.

Opera's Voices: From Translation to Transfiguration

Whereas Whitman's poetic ear was attuned to and translating the voice of Romantic opera, Kate Chopin discovered an equally compelling source of emotional power and transcendence in Wagnerian operas. Wagner's performance innovations (darkened theater, silent audience) presuppose the transcendent power of opera's "voices" and refocus the attention of the audience on the artistic performance and not the class-based aspirations of the cultural phenomena of opera. In Wagner's opera *Tristan and Isolde,* Kate Chopin encountered the seduction of sound, a Whitmanesque voice that "speaks to the soul" (Chopin, *The Awakening* 15). Wagnerian opera provided Chopin with a model of and language for describing a transformation of self that is also a transfiguration of the soul.

Embracing Whitman and Chopin's emphasis on the solitary nature of aesthetic experience, Willa Cather equated the voice with the literal and physical voice of the opera singer. For Cather, the diva portrayed perfectly the power and the plight of the female artist. When Phineas T. Barnum brought the Swedish Nightingale—Jenny Lind—to New York in 1850, he introduced America to the star quality of a diva. According to Dizikes's account, the soprano's tour of America made art "familiar" and "unthreatening" (133). Her American tour helped counter the opposition to opera that nationalism had created, and "success came more and more to be fixed in box-office terms" (Dizikes 130). Having raised the public's anticipation of her visit with extensive publicity, Barnum promoted her by "escort[ing] Jenny Lind and her companion in his private barouche" (Morris 59). The public's hunger for information about Lind prompted the creation of a new form of newspaper reporting: the interview (real or supposed) with an artist. The interview "increased—often created—familiarity with a performer otherwise unknown. It reduced the distance between the reader and the great star" (Morris 136). In his essay "Jenny Lind and the Voice of America," Lowell Gallagher explains the crucial role that Lind served in transforming the image of the prima donna:

> Indeed, the public required, [. . .] that the prima donna who enacted the part of the long-suffering female victim be nothing less than, quite literally, a *casta diva,*[5] a chaste, even disembodied, goddess able to transcend the dross of earthly experience. In her nineteenth-century American tour, her audience looked to Lind to provide them with a quasi-religious experience that would, through the magical power of her desexualized body and voice, heal the social divisions of the nation. In the case of Lind, who made every attempt to fulfill her devotee's expectations, the playful perversity of opera's gender-bent past gives way to a fetishistic mode of diva-worship. (13)

Suggesting that the diva possesses a divine artistic power (which borders on madness), Louisa May Alcott's "The Rival Prima Donnas" anticipates many of the themes that Willa Cather would explore extensively in her short stories and novels. The diva, or "goddess," possesses the power of divine inspiration, and through her body, her voice, and her passion, she embodies the artistic ideal. Her voice, like art, exemplifies two paradoxical traits: eternality and temporality. The art that she creates will outlast the instrument of her artistic expression: her voice. Alcott's dueling divas also illustrate what Susan McClary calls the "musical representation of madwomen"—both on the stage and off it. By choosing a bel canto opera (*Norma*) for the divas to sing, Alcott capitalizes on the excesses of the music Bellini wrote for the lead soprano. As McClary explains, "In opera, the madwoman is given the music of greatest stylistic privilege, the music that seems to do what is most quintessentially musical, as opposed to verbal or conventional. She is a pretext for compositional misbehavior" (102). With vocal embellishments, the soprano in a bel canto opera sings to her undoing.[6]

Cather bridges the gap between American writers' divided attention to opera. Like Whitman, Chopin, and Alcott, Cather emphasizes the importance of voice, but she also inherits another interpretive strand—an attention to the cultural context of opera. The art form could not be divorced from its cultural context, one infused with display, consumption, and commodification. Edgar Allan Poe anticipates this focus on opera's spaces in the middle of the nineteenth century.

Opera's Reverberations in Space

Unlike Whitman, Poe left no definitive record in letters or journal entries of the operas he attended. While living in New York in 1845, however, Poe worked for the *Broadway Journal,* first serving as assistant editor and later as editor and proprietor. While working at the journal, Poe would have attended and reviewed numerous theatrical performances, including operatic ones. The original publisher, John Bisco, promised, "The *Broadway Journal* will differ from any of the weekly Periodicals now published in this city, as it will be made up entirely of original matter, consisting of Essays, Criticisms on Art and Literature, and Literary and Scientific Intelligence" (16). In addition to giving announcements of upcoming operatic performances, including listing venues, works, composers, and performers, each edition of the weekly publication featured reviews. Although the reviews were unsigned, Poe certainly wrote some of them.

Poe's tenure at the journal included the years that Davis's New Orleans troupe performed in New York. The June 28, 1845, edition includes a review of the French Opera Company's performance at the Park Theatre. In addition to discussing the artistic merits of the performance, the editor discusses his concern about the price of admission—something that would have been particularly relevant for Poe, a man plagued by monetary troubles throughout his life. As the reviewer states: "One thing we should strongly urge upon Mr. Davis, namely, the absolute necessity of lowering the price of admission to the pit, from one dollar to fifty cents. [. . .] There are hundreds of young men who would willingly go to the Opera every performing night, but who will not pay a dollar, and will not go up stairs to the second tier, and so stay away altogether" ("French Opera" 410). Not coincidentally, in the same year that he began working for the *Broadway Journal,* Poe published "The Spectacles" in the November 22 edition. As his short story illustrates, Poe's exposure to the opera had an impact on his fiction.

Interested in the architecture of opera, Poe locates his narrative in the opera house. His interest in opera's physicality extends beyond the embodied presence of the singers to the opera house as a space of spectacle. From the Italian term *grottesca,* "grotto-ish," the word grotesque originally served as an architectural description. Poe relies upon the architecture of opera to create his grotesque tale, "The Spectacles" (1844). When Whitman alludes to opera, he rarely places the singer within the confines of an opera house. Instead, he hears the operatic voices in nature, creating a harmony between music and the natural world. In contrast, Poe places opera in the context of performance. The physical setting allows the writer to explore the significance of theatrical convention and social propriety. Using opera to frame his narrative, Poe traces the connection between vision and vanity. As Poe's title suggests, the vision of his main character is literally impaired. A place where one simultaneously views a performance and participates in public display, the opera house provides an ideal setting for this tale. Both Poe's theme and his focus on opera's spaces find further development in the work of James and Wharton. They, too, explore the multifaceted significance of opera's physical confines.

In the cosmopolitan world of Henry James and Edith Wharton, opera functioned as both a commodity and a standard of custom and convention. Descended from socially established families, James and Wharton were particularly suited to critique the tastes and forms of the American upper class. For these aristocrats, opera represented "all the elements of the cosmopolitan spirit of the European capitals by itself" (Tintner, *Cosmopolitan World* 302). As demonstrated in their fiction, Wharton and James understood the significance of such an implication. Discussing New York's "extravagant insistence on the Opera" in *The American Scene*, James describes "the oddest sense of hearing it, as an institution, groan and creak, positively almost split and crack, with the extra weight thrown upon it—the weight that in worlds otherwise arranged and artfully scattered, distributed over all the ground" (117–18). James and Wharton not only considered opera as a benchmark of taste and form but also explored the significance of the opera box as a space for social rituals of rejection and privilege and as a location of spectacle and display.

As the nineteenth century neared its close, opera gradually infiltrated even the small-town opera houses of middle America, moving from the East Coast westward and extending beyond the confines of the privileged. America's attention, however, was divided. The expansion of opera's audience is reflected in the appearance of opera in a diverse cross section of American literature. Writers from Whitman to Wharton found the art form uniquely suited to the American canvas. For some, opera provided a powerful artistic medium for expressing a private aesthetic experience. Writers like Walt Whitman, Kate Chopin, Louisa May Alcott, and Willa Cather recognized that the artifice and convention of opera did not detract from its ability to illustrate unbridled passion and emotion. In opera, they discovered the embodied voice of the artist. Others, like Edgar Allan Poe, Henry James, and Edith Wharton found the spectacle of opera as well as its spaces, the opera houses and boxes, perfectly suited for displaying the class-based and commodity-driven aspirations of America's new aristocracy.

1

EMBODYING POETIC TRANSCENDENCE

Whitman and Opera

Leaves of Grass, first published the week of Independence Day in 1855 by the author himself, represents Walt Whitman's attempt to answer Emerson's call for an authentic and distinctly American poetry. As John Townsend Trowbridge reports, Whitman "freely admitted that he could never have written his poems if he had not first 'come to himself,' and that Emerson helped him to 'find himself'" (166). As Whitman so memorably phrased the matter, "I was simmering, simmering, simmering; Emerson brought me to a boil" (qtd. in Trowbridge 166). Acknowledging his debt to Emerson, Whitman boldly expressed confidence when he sent a copy to his mentor, eager for his response and affirmation. Whitman's poetry echoed the ideals that would come to be associated with an American identity: self-reliance, democratic equality, ingenuity, and diversity. He celebrates the grandeur and variety of the natural landscape and the human inhabitants of America. Taking *Leaves of Grass* through nine editions, from its initial publication in 1855 to the final one in 1891, he remained committed to singing the "choral music of democracy" (Dizikes 184). Whitman reflected on his work in "A Backward Glance O'er Travel'd Roads," in the 1889 edition of *Leaves of Grass:*

> Plenty of songs had been sung—beautiful, matchless songs—adjusted to other lands than these—another spirit and stage of evolution; but I would sing, and leave out or put in, quite solely with reference to America and to-day. Modern science

> and democracy seem'd to be throwing out their challenge to poetry to put them in its statements in contradistinction to the songs and myths of the past. As I see it now (perhaps too late,) I have unwittingly taken up that challenge and made an attempt at such statements—which I certainly would not assume to do now, knowing more clearly what it means. (*Leaves of Grass* 563–64)

Whitman, in fact, discovered his "meter-making argument" (Emerson 220) in the rhythms of music, particularly Italian opera.

Although not a musician himself, Whitman recognized the beauty and value of music, and he did not believe that an appreciation of music belonged solely to the wealthy or to the elite. Keeping true to the spirit of American democracy, Whitman desired to "spread a capacity and fondness of music among the masses" in order "to refine and polish them in the truest sense" (*Gathering* 358). As the editor of the *Brooklyn Daily Eagle*, he published his sentiments about the vital role of music in the public education of American children: "It were well if music were made a regular branch of study in all our common schools. The meliorating influence of such a practice on the minds and habits of youth is beyond dispute—and indeed, with the exception of New York, nearly all the schools of the land *do* sing" (*Gathering* 358). A year later, on September 8, 1847, Whitman underscored his earlier comments about the importance of music in the nation's civic life: "The subtlest spirit of a nation is expressed through its music—and the music acts reciprocally upon the nation's very soul. [. . .] But no human power can thoroughly suppress the spirit which lives in national lyrics, and sounds in the favorite melodies sung by high and low" (*Gathering* 345–46).

Initially, Whitman favored "the music of feeling—heart music as distinguished from art music," dismissing what he referred to as the "stale, second hand, foreign method, with its flourishes, its ridiculous sentimentality, its anti-republican spirit, and its sycophantic tainting [of] the young taste of the nation" (*Gathering* 347–48). In disparaging Italian opera, he merely echoed the prevailing opinion of other journalists and reviewers of his day. When the first Italian opera came to New York in 1825, the reviewers at the *New-York Literary Gazette and*

Phi Beta Kappa Repository asked, "Is the false Italian school of opera natural? What man ever *sung* out his fit of passion? Who in jealousy, ambition, or revenge, ever vented his feelings in song? No man: on the contrary, these passions always destroy the harmony of the mind, and often choke the utterance" ("The Opera" 239). But Whitman eventually discovered an authentic American voice within these foreign forms, too. He learned that music may function simultaneously as "the distinguishing ornament of fashionable society and more the harmonizing and spiritualizing force in a heterogeneous but democratic society" (Cooke 225).

Although Whitman admired various musical forms, it was not until he discovered opera that he found a suitable medium for the transcendent power of American poetry. In opera, Whitman identified an authentic voice for expressing human emotion and experience. His immersion in opera began as a vocational necessity. In the years prior to composing *Leaves of Grass*, reviewing performances for the journals exposed him to numerous operas. In addition to the New York performances his pressman's pass allowed him, Whitman also experienced opera during his visit to New Orleans.[1] From the Eastern seaboard to the Southern gulf, Whitman heard and saw some of the finest European and American singers and opera companies. In an excerpt from "Specimen Days," entitled "Plays and Operas too," Whitman chronicles many performances, and he connects these experiences with the "gestation of *Leaves of Grass*" (*Complete* 4: 24).

> All through the years, off and on, I frequented [. . .] the Italian operas at Chambers-street, Astor Place or the Battery—many seasons was on the free list, writing for papers even as quite a youth! [. . .] I heard, these years, well render'd, all the Italian and other operas in vogue, "Sonnambula," "The Puritans," "Der Freischutz," "Huguenots," "Fille du Regiment," "Faust," "Étoile du Nord," "Poliuto," and others. Verdi's "Ernani," "Rigoletto," and "Trovatore," with Donnizetti's [*sic*] "Lucia" or "Favorita" or "Lucrezia," and Auber's "Massaniello," or Rossini's "William Tell" and "Gazza Ladra," were among my special enjoyments. I heard Alboni every time she sang in New York and vicinity—

> also Grisi, the tenor Mario, and the baritone Badiali, the finest in the world. (*Complete* 4: 24–26)

Walt Whitman's musical tastes came of age with the explosion of opera in New York: "By good luck his journalistic days in Brooklyn and New York coincided with one of the golden moments in the history of opera in this country," Robert Faner relates, "a moment when the musical fashion insisted upon a type of opera in which the voices of singers were displayed as never before or since, and a moment when singers of heroic stature had miraculously appeared to perform" (228).

Even during the chaos of the Civil War, Whitman continued to seek opera as a source of pleasure and amusement. In 1863, Whitman worked in a war hospital in Washington, D.C., but he periodically returned home to Brooklyn and attended the opera. In his diary, Whitman recalled that he went to Brooklyn on November 2, and on November 4 he viewed a production of *Lucrezia Borgia*, featuring Medori, Mazzoleni, and Bianchi, who offered a "very fine" performance. A few nights later, Whitman returned to the opera. The entry for that day reads, "November 16. Opera. Wrote to Ellen O'Connor" (qtd. in Glicksberg 139). That same month, Whitman wrote to some soldiers he had befriended in Washington, describing the performance of *Lucrezia Borgia* as a moving experience. After offering a brief synopsis of the plot, he continues:

> Comrades, recollect all this (the action of the opera) is in singing and music, and lots of it too, on a big scale, in the band, every instrument you can think of, and the best players in the world, and sometimes the whole band and the whole men's chorus and the women's chorus all putting the steam together—and all in a vast house, light as day, and with a crowded audience of ladies and men. Such singing and strong music always give me the greatest pleasure—and so the opera is the only amusement I have gone to, for my own satisfaction, for the last ten years. (qtd. in Traubel 3: 104)

Even after Whitman's job of reviewing opera was over, he sought the art form for pleasure. *Leaves of Grass* and the opera incubated in Whitman's imagination simultaneously.

Whitman's first critical review of an opera appeared on March 23, 1847, in the *Brooklyn Daily Eagle.* Incidentally, the production that Whitman reviewed, *The Barber of Seville,* was the same production that had christened opera's entry into New York's cultural world in 1825. Whitman's review suggests his familiarity with the opera and the individual singers. "Although this production of Rossini's is familiar, it is nevertheless always heard with pleasure: the instrumentation is beautiful, and has that clean, though rather old fashioned character, in which his delicate ideas produce effect, and not any overpowering crash of instruments" (*Gathering* 350). In an article published in the November 10, 1855, edition of *Life Illustrated,* "The Opera," Whitman articulates the powerful effect of this musical medium.

> You listen to this music, and the songs, and choruses—all of the highest range of composition known to the world of melody. It is novel, of course, being far, very far different from what you were used to—the church choir, or the songs and playing on the piano, or the nigger songs, or any performance of the Ethiopian minstrels, or the concerts of the different "families." A new world—a liquid world—rushes like a torrent through you. If you have the true musical feeling in you, from this night you date a new era in your development, and, for the first time, receive your ideas of what the divine art of music really is. Every thing these players and singers do is so much broader, sweeter, firmer. If you are a vocalist, you see you did not previously know how to even open your mouth. You did not know how to express the simplest sounds properly. These singers do it all so much easier, and incomparably better. This is science! This is art! You envy Italy, and almost become an enthusiast; you wish an equal art here, and an equal science and style, underlain by a perfect understanding of American realities, and the appropriateness of our national spirit and body also. (*New York* 22)

His exposure to opera as a journalist trained him in the skill of articulating the merits of a performance's particulars—the players, the singers, the setting, the audience; however, Whitman's analysis went beyond these mere details. As his description illustrates, he also possessed a keen interest in vocal technique. By analyzing and admiring the method that singers used to control their bodies—their mouths, their vocal chords, their diaphragms—Whitman discovers an embodied source of creative energy and poetic expression.

Whitman's response to these operas extends beyond an emotional one. While he worked on composing the poems for *Leaves of Grass*, he pondered the invaluable link between the hybrid art form he listened to and observed on the stage and the art he produced in his own writing. John Irwin explains that "for Whitman the interplay (of Apollonian image and Dionysian music in opera) is always figurative. Neither a composer of music nor a writer of opera, Whitman had only words with which to achieve that interplay of visual presence and musical immediacy that is meant to solve the inadequacy of words" (191). As a hybrid form, opera incorporated a variety of expressive forms into one art. With elements of music, drama, dance, and poetry, it represents a multi-layered canvas of self-expression. "In attempting to raise words to the condition of music," as Irwin notes (191), Whitman located his poetic self-expression in the human voice. Long a student of oratory, he understood the power of vocal expression. In "Some Laggards Yet," Whitman considers "The Perfect Human Voice": "Beyond all other power and beauty, there is something in the quality and power of the right voice (*timbre* the schools call it) that touches the soul, the abysms" (*Complete* 7: 21). Among those Whitman identifies as "celebrated people possessing this wonderful vocal power," he includes the contralto Alboni and the tenor Bettini. Whitman ponders the possibility that "the best philosophy and poetry, or something like the best, after all these centuries, perhaps waits to be rous'd out yet, or suggested, by the perfect physiological human voice" (*Complete* 7: 22). In these early articulations of the role of the human voice, he reveals the touchstone for his poetic perception: the singing voice.

In opera, Whitman discovered the medium ideally designed for displaying and relating the vast power and diversity of vocal expression. As his catalog illustrates, Whitman favored romantic, bel canto

Italian operas, characterized by ornamentation, vocal flourishes, and frills. The composer allows the individual singer the opportunity to display vocal prowess and style. In *The Angel's Cry: Beyond the Pleasure Principle,* Michel Poizat traces the development of opera as naturally leading to the vocal thrills that Whitman admires: "It does not seem unreasonable to look upon the history of opera as a long progression that begins with speech, sung as closely as possible to the phrasing of spoken language; covers a trajectory in which singing grows more and more detached from speech and tends more and more toward the high notes; and culminates in the pure cry" (40). Finding in opera an inspiration for poetic perception and translation, Whitman introduced a fresh, new voice into American poetry. He "sings" and "celebrates" the power of the human voice, a voice intimately connected to the human body and to nature: "I am the poet of the Body and I am the poet of the Soul, / The pleasures of heaven are with me and the pains of hell are with me, / The first I graft and increase upon myself, the latter I translate into a new tongue" ("Song of Myself," lines 422–24). The tongue, or voice, that Whitman uses to translate his perceptions is a singing voice. "At opera's moments of intense erotic fulfillment," explains Sam Abel, "the singer becomes pure voice; the body, the scenery, everything other than the voice of the singer disappears from consciousness; and we in the audience become one with the ecstatic cry of the unmediated voice" (46). The subsequent physical responses to this stimulus awaken a range of reactions: pain, pleasure, rage, sorrow, and joy.

"My voice goes after what my eyes cannot reach," Whitman explains in "Song of Myself"; "With the twirl of my tongue I encompass worlds and volumes of worlds. / Speech is the twin of my vision, it is unequal to measure itself" (lines 564–66). As many of the later poems in *Leaves of Grass* also illustrate, vision and voice are closely related. In "Song of Myself," Whitman asserts, "Writing and talk do not prove me." Instead, he "will do nothing for a long time but listen, / And accrue what [he] hear[s] into this song, . . . to let sounds contribute toward [him]" (lines 579, 582–83). Whitman goes on to catalog all the various noises he encounters, harmonizing those of the city, of the human voice, and of nature. All these reverberations together create a "chorus," a "grand opera" that "suits" Whitman's ears (line 599).

The climax of the sounds, however, is two human voices—a "tenor large and fresh as the creation" and "the trained soprano" who "convulses me like the climax of my love-grip" (lines 601, 603). The power of these voices invokes a physical response that surpasses passive listening. In *Bodily Charm: Living Opera*, Linda and Michael Hutcheon explore the "physical dimensions of the art form—singer's bodies, spectator's bodies, but also dramatized representations of bodies" (xiii). Like Whitman, the Hutcheons recognize the vital role of the body in experiencing opera: "In short, your body is very busy at the opera. Writing about staged theater, Marvin Carlson reminds us that the roots of the words 'theatre' (from *theatron*, a place for seeing), 'spectator' (from *spectare*, to watch), and 'auditorium' (from *audire*, to hear) all reflect the necessary physicality and presence of the theatre experience" (154). In "Song of Myself," Whitman describes the range of responses to hearing operatic voices:

> It wrenches such ardors from me I did not know I possess'd them,
> It sails me, I dab with bare feet, they are lick'd by the indolent waves,
> I am cut by bitter and angry hail, I lose my breath,
> Steep'd amid honey'd morphine, my windpipe throttled in fakes of death [. . .]. (lines 605–8)

While Whitman's focus on the human body and sexuality in his poetry was considered sensational by many of his contemporaries, this focus is not what uniquely distinguishes Whitman's use of operatic form.[2] Whitman occasionally uses orgasmic metaphors in *Leaves of Grass* to describe the powerful response of the listener to an opera singer's voice, but it is the poet's translation of those sounds—not his physical response—that provides the most innovative use of opera in Whitman's poetry. The orgasmic language that Whitman uses to describe the experience of listening to opera merely imitates a composer's seduction of the audience through music that "carries the burden of sexual discourse" (Abel 105). Musicologist Susan McClary explains that "tonality itself—with its process of instilling expectations and subsequently withholding promised fulfillment until climax—is the principal musical means during the period from 1600–1900 for arousing and channeling desire" (12). Trained in the patterns of Western tonality, most opera audiences will be seduced by the tension, and, ultimately, the resolution of the musical orgasms that composers include in their works.

Not only does the spectator experience a bodily reaction to an operatic performance, but the singers, too, undergo a physical response. A singer's voice is "a physically embodied instrument, one that is endowed with a motor, a vibrator, and a resonator. Or, to use another metaphor, it is like a wind instrument: it has bellows (the lungs), a windpipe (the bronchi and trachea), a reed (the vocal cords), resonators (the closed cavities in the cranium and face), and a speaking trumpet: (the mouth)" (Hutcheon and Hutcheon 125). While the sounds produced by this embodied voice assist the spectator in transcending a bodily existence, they are grounded in the physical presence of the singer. Despite the vital importance of bodily response to Whitman's metaphorical use of opera, these references should not diminish the significance of the poet's translation of the voice that produced the reaction in its listener. The initial physical reaction triggers the poet's awareness of his ability to interpret and translate the sounds his ears receive.

Whitman recognizes that the heightened perception or the ecstasy of the poet is worthless until translated into a song that the common man may sing. Conveying the transformational power of his initial physical response to opera, Whitman creates a voice capable of celebrating the ability of every man and woman to participate in the song of democracy.

> By opera Whitman was first lifted to the heights of mystical rapture wherein he realized that he was a poet with a poet's message for the world. Following this inspiration came the recognition that in opera lay the elements of a technique which would enable the "outsetting bard" to present his message in a manner which could preserve its largeness and naturalness, which would not destroy its inspirational power by cloaking it with forms of artificiality and pettiness, and which, inciden-

> tally, would be exactly appropriate for the great new land which he was to celebrate. (Faner 85)

In "Vocalism," Whitman considers the poet's power: "Vocalism, measure, concentration, determination, and the divine power to speak words" (line 1). This divinity is not attributed indiscriminately to every voice. Instead, the poet "waits for the right voices," the "practis'd and perfect organ," the "develop'd soul" (lines 16–17). In his prose and his poetry, Whitman identifies this voice with opera singers. "The Dead Tenor," a tribute to Signor Pasquale Brignoli, credits the mourned tenor with having had the "perfect singing voice" that "through those strains distill'd—how the rapt ears, the soul of me, absorbing / *Fernando's* heart, *Manrico's* passionate call, *Ernani's,* sweet *Gennaro's*" (lines 7–8). Through the one voice, Pasquale's voice, Whitman hears the language of various emotions and characters. In his ode, the poet describes the singer as "seek[ing] to fold, within [his] chants transmuting, / Freedom's and Love's and Faith's unloos'd cantabile" ("The Dead Tenor" lines 9–10).

In his prose, Whitman expresses the same sentiment: "Have not you, in like manner, while listening to the well-played music of some band like Maretzek's, felt an overwhelming desire for measureless sound—a sublime orchestra of a myriad orchestras—a colossal volume of harmony, in which the thunder might roll in its proper place; and above it, the vast, pure Tenor—identity of the Creative Power itself—rising through the universe, until the boundless and unspeakable capacities of that mystery, the human soul, should be filled to the uttermost, and the problem of human cravingness be satisfied and destroyed?" (*Uncollected* 1: 256). In this same letter, Whitman goes on to praise "those fresh vigorous tones of Bettini!" Whitman claimed that Bettini's "voice has often affected me to tears. Its clear, firm, wonderfully exalting notes, filling and expanding away; dwelling like a poised lark up in heaven; have made my very soul tremble" (257). These individual artists provide the vehicle for a transcendent experience. By transporting the poet to a higher plane of perception and emotion, the singer's voice translates the inarticulate language of the universe into a song that the poet may transcribe for all of humanity. Whitman invites us to listen: "Pure and vast, that voice now rises, as on clouds, to the heaven where it claims audience. Now, firm and unbroken, it spreads like an ocean around us. Ah, welcome that I know not the mere language of the earthly words in which the melody is embodied; as all words are mean before the language of true music" (*Uncollected* 1: 258–59).

In addition to idolizing the male voices of Brignoli, Bettini, and Badiali, he also greatly admired Madame Marietta Alboni. She appeared in ten operas during the New York season of 1852–1853, and Whitman acknowledges attending all of these performances. In fact, he recalls: "I heard Alboni every time she sang in New York and vicinity [. . .]" (*Complete* 1: 26). One of the poems included in the 1860 edition of *Leaves of Grass*, "To a Certain Cantatrice," serves as Whitman's tribute to Alboni. The five lines of the poem reveal the power that the bard places in the voice of the opera singer:

> Here take this gift,
> I was reserving it for some hero, some speaker, or general,
> One who should serve the good old cause, the great idea, the
>   progress and freedom of the race,
> Some brave comforter of despots, some daring rebel;
> But I see that what I was reserving belongs to you just as much
>   as to any.

In the voice of an opera singer, Whitman recognizes heroism, nobility, beauty, and equality—all characteristics he associated with the young American nation in *Leaves of Grass*. In an account dated Tuesday, August 21, 1888, Whitman recalls his perceived golden age of opera: "Oh! Those great days! great, great days! Alboni, Badiali, [the superbest of all superb baritones in my time] in particular: no one can tell, know, even suspect, how much they had to do with the making of *Leaves of Grass*" (Traubel 2: 173–74). The voices of opera struck a permanent chord in the bard's imagination and intellect. All of his subsequent work reflects an awareness of the singing voice in all creation.

Whitman asserts the discovery of his own poetic voice; he describes himself as singing. The poem that demonstrates this transformation most explicitly is the celebrated "Out of the Cradle Endlessly Rocking," which appeared in the 1860 edition of *Leaves of Grass*. The poet sings his "reminiscence" about a time "when the lilac-scent was in the air and the Fifth-month grass was growing" (lines 22, 24), and he, a "curious boy," observes "two feather'd guests from Alabama" without "disturbing them, / Cautiously peering, absorbing, translating" (lines 29, 26, 31). His encounter with these two birds transforms the child into a poet capable of translating the sounds of nature for humanity. Listening to the mournful "aria" (line 130) of the he-bird, the child gradually realizes that he, unlike most men, not only hears the notes emanating from the bird's vocal chords but also understands the content of the songs.

In an effort to differentiate the bird's songs from the boy's thoughts, Whitman italicizes the bird's mournful song. Essentially, he transcribes the music of an aria into written words. The libretto for most Italian romantic operas already appears in poetic form, but when Whitman translates the he-bird's aria, he interprets a language foreign to any other person. He relies not only on his ears to interpret the sounds but also on his inner being: "The aria's meaning, the ears, the soul, swiftly depositing" (line 138). By identifying the bird's song as an aria, Whitman reveals his immersion in operatic concepts. In operatic convention, an aria refers to a solo number that extends a single emotion throughout the piece. Rather than involving a dialogue with other characters or facilitating the forward movement of the action in an opera, an aria captures a moment in time. The aria allows the singer the opportunity to reveal his emotions to the audience. The bird's aria unveils the mystery of life and death to the young poet. The child recognizes his own keen sensitivity to the voices and passions that pulse within the universe. The bard describes the recognition of his transformation in the following lines:

> O you singer solitary, singing by yourself, projecting me,
> O solitary me listening, never more shall I cease perpetuating
>   you,
> Never more shall I escape, never more the reverberations,
> Never more the cries of unsatisfied love be absent from me,
> Never again leave me to be the peaceful child I was before what
>   there in the night,
> By the sea under the yellow and sagging moon,

> The messenger there arous'd, the fire, the sweet hell within,
> The unknown want, the destiny of me. (lines 150–57)

From that moment forward, the young boy assumes the role of the bard. As he explains: "Now in a moment I know what I am for, I awake" (line 147).

In several of his prose writings, Whitman compares the voice of an opera singer to that of a bird. Hearing Anna Bishop perform the role of Lucia in Gaetano Donizetti's *Lucia di Lammermoor* reminded him of the "gyrations of birds in air" (Whitman, *Gathering* 352). Listening to the coloratura soprano sing the trills and ornaments while playfully dancing with the woodwinds during her famous mad scene caused "a new world—a liquid world—[to] rush like a torrent through" the listener (Whitman, *New York* 22). Whitman describes Bishop's voice as "the purest soprano—and of as silvery clearness as ever came from the human throat—rich, but not massive—and of such flexibility that one is almost appalled at the way the most difficult passages are not only gone over with ease, but actually dallied with, and their difficulty redoubled" (*Gathering* 351–52). While many listeners will recognize in Donizetti's score the intentional imitation of a bird's chirping in this aria, Whitman hears the sounds not as the jumbled and inarticulate musings of a mad woman; instead, he translates the emanations of the voice into emotions and passions that may be felt and understood by the listener. In a letter written in Brooklyn, dated November 8, 1863, Whitman addresses his "dear comrades in the hospital" with these words: "The opera here now has some of the greatest singers in the world—the principal lady singer (her name is Medori) has a voice that would make you hold your breath with wonder and delight—it is like a miracle—no mocking bird or clearest flute can begin with it [. . .]" (Traubel 3: 103).

In his poems, he seamlessly weaves together the voices of nature, of instruments, and of human beings, creating a "Tutti! for earth and heaven" allowing "man and art and Nature [to be] fused again" ("Proud Music of the Storm," lines 52, 51). Whitman most clearly expresses this fusion of voices in "Proud Music of the Storm," which he first published in the *Atlantic Monthly* in 1869. Included in the 1871 edition of *Leaves of Grass*, the poem describes the "Blending with Nature's rhythmus all the tongues of nations" (line 6). Whitman begins with the "hidden orchestras" (line 4) of nature's prairies, forest treetops, and mountains, then moves to the sounds of composers, organs, instruments, and voices. His words demonstrate the blending of these various types of music:

> Now the great organ sounds,
> [. . .] And with it every instrument in multitudes,
> The players playing, all the world's musicians,
> The solemn hymns and masses rousing adoration,
> All passionate heart-chants, sorrowful appeals,
> The measureless sweet vocalists of ages,
> And for their solvent setting earth's own diapason,
> Of winds and woods and mighty ocean waves,
> A new composite orchestra, binder of years and climes, ten-fold
> renewer [. . .]. (lines 33, 40–47)

In the third section of the poem, Whitman articulates a theory of how voice influences the poet.

> Ah from a little child,
> Thou knowest soul how to me all sounds became music,
> My mother's voice in lullaby or hymn,
> (The voice, O tender voices, memory's loving voices,
> Last miracle of all, O dearest mother's, sister's, voices). (lines
> 59–63)

He intuitively understands that the first voice he hears is his mother's—even before his birth. By identifying these sounds with his mother's voice, he learns to associate "speech with presence, the presence of the living voice, the evident context, the meaningful intonation, etc., while writing represents the absence of all that," explains John Irwin (181). He observes that the "poet, a writer of phonetic script whose poetic self consists of that very script, faces, then, a double absence in the use of phonetic signs—the absence both of live speaking voice and of the referent" (Irwin 181). In music, however, Whitman provides a mode of recovering the speaking voice—even on the written page.

"Whitman's making the self the sole referent of the poem necessarily involves his identifying the poem/self with music," Irwin says, "for what Pater meant when he said that all art aspires to the condition of music (that condition in which 'the end is not distinct from the means, the form from the matter, the subject from the expression') is that all art aspires to the self-referentiality of the Romantic self, the self as pure will, as pure motion/emotion" (184). This recognition of the earliest voice as the maternal one connects Whitman to Wordsworth and the Romantic tradition established in *The Prelude.* Wordsworth describes the influence of the mother's voice in this way:

> From early days,
> Beginning not long after that first time
> In which, a Babe, by intercourse of touch
> I held mute dialogues with my Mother's heart,
> I have endeavored to display the means
> Whereby the infant sensibility,
> Great birthright of our Being, was in me
> Augmented and sustained. (2.281–87)

By choosing the words "intercourse" and "dialogues," Wordsworth characterizes the mother's embrace as a communicative exchange. The "Mother's eye" and the infant's gaze share in a powerful, internal conversation. Despite the infant's inability to speak audible tones, he and the mother understand one another implicitly. The heart of the mother relays the thoughts and feelings to the child's own sensibility. While Wordsworth focuses on the mother's gaze, Whitman emphasizes the mother's actual voice. Both poets recognize that the earliest modes of human communication are established in the maternal-infant bond, but Whitman hears that bond as a melodic voice that inspires his own audible response.

Recent scholars rely on Freud's and Lacan's psychoanalytic theories to assess the mother's influence in an infant's language acquisition. According to those who study child development, a newborn infant experiences a period of "primary identification, aptly emphasizing the infant's object cathexis of someone it does not yet differentiate from its self" (Chodorow 61). Following this primary identification period, the infant moves to the "symbiotic" state of "mother-child dual unity" (Chodorow 61). These stages of physiological and psychological development suggest that the infant does not possess the ability to communicate with the mother because he does not perceive her as a separate entity. The duality of an infant's early identity allows theorists like Freud and Lacan the opportunity to explain why and how the child learns to distinguish himself from another. In the "Lacanian myth of language acquisition" (a label applied by Margaret Homans), in the preoedipal stage the "child shares with the mother what Julia Kristeva calls the semiotic, consisting of body language and nonrepresentational sounds" (Homans 6), an unmediated mode of communication. According to Lacan, language skills are acquired as the child becomes aware of sexual difference with the mother. Identifying language with the patriarchal system of symbols, the infant begins to develop his own masculine identification. By suggesting the necessity of separation from the mother, these theories invite a consideration of the mother's absence as well as her presence in the infant's life. This shift in focus has prompted many Wordsworth scholars to concentrate on the significance of the mother's death and on the poet's need to replace the absent mother with another figure: nature. While Whitman follows in Wordsworth's tradition of using nature as powerful presence in his poetry, he chooses instead to focus on a human expression: the music of opera. Rather than having to choose between the gaze and the voice, Whitman discovers a means of recovering both. Just as his earliest connection with language came through the mother's gaze and voice, Whitman's interactions with opera offer him an unmediated access to both human physical presence and an audible voice.

By drawing upon opera in his poetry, Whitman establishes an effective method of speaking through words—with a living voice. "For Whitman, poetic singing and poetic seeing are a mutually constitutive opposition, and throughout the poems the words 'I sing' and 'I see' constantly give way to one another in an oscillating equivalency" (192), claims Irwin. Even as Whitman praises the music of nature, he recalls "Italia's peerless compositions" ("Proud Music of the Storm," line 75), the operas whose heroes and heroines inspired an awakening of his soul. At the conclusion of the third section of "Proud Music of the Storm," the bard recalls the visions and sounds of the opera, punctuated by the phrases "I see" and "I hear":

> Across the stage with pallor on her face, yet lurid passion,
> Stalks Norma brandishing the dagger in her hand.
>
> I see poor crazed Lucia's eyes' unnatural gleam,
> Her hair down her back falls loose and dishevel'd.
>
> I see where Ernani walking the bridal garden,
> Amid the scent of night-roses, radiant, holding his bride by the
>   hand,
> Hears the infernal call, the death-pledge of the horn.
>
> To crossing swords and gray hairs bared to heaven,
> The clear electric base and baritone of the world,
> The trombone duo, Libertad forever!
> From Spanish chestnut trees' dense shade,
> By old and heavy convent walls a wailing song,
> Song of lost love, the torch of youth and life quench'd in de-
>   spair,
> Song of the dying swan, Fernando's heart is breaking.
>
> Awaking from her woes at last retriev'd Amina sings,
> Copious as stars and glad as morning light the torrents of her
>   joy.
>
> (The teeming lady comes,
> The lustrious orb, Venus contralto, the blooming mother,
> Sister of loftiest gods, Alboni's self I hear). (lines 76–94)

Once again Whitman experiences the "seeing" and "singing" simultaneously at the opera.

The operas he refers to in "Proud Music of the Storm" involve the overwhelming passion of love, the tragedy of suicide and death, and the rage of madness and revenge. Just as the young boy perceived and internalized the sea's "hissing melodious" of the "low and delicious word death" (lines 170, 168) in "Out of the Cradle Endlessly Rocking," the speaker in "Proud Music of the Storm" "hears" and "sees" the agonies of Norma, Lucia, Ernani, Fernando, and Amina through the voices and actions of the opera singers. By merging the operatic echoes of life and death with the reverberations of nature that express the bridge between the mortal and immortal world,[3] Whitman claims the expansive calling of the bard: "Give me to hold all sounds (I madly struggling cry,) / Fill me with all the voices of the universe" (lines 138–39). For Whitman, the music of the storm includes the voices of nature, of instruments, of human voices. As Krause observes, "Significantly, the original title of the poem was *Proud Music of the Sea-Storm.* As we know, the sea symbolized Whitman's conception of the cosmic life processes. [. . .] When Whitman revised *Proud Music* (at the same time deleting 'Sea' from the title)," Krause continues, "he reinforced his original idea by inserting the key phrase 'bridging the way from Life to death,' to describe the new poems he wanted to write" (710). The music of the universe harmonizes in Whitman's ears to create "Poems bridging the way from Life to Death, vaguely wafted in night air, uncaught, unwritten, / Which let us go forth in the bold day and write" (lines 163–64).

This "new bard caroling in the West" strives to facilitate a distinctly American melody with his poetry. Focusing on this American identity in operatic expression, Whitman writes "Italian Music in Dakota," one of the new poems included in the 1881 edition of *Leaves of Grass.* This poem illustrates his totalizing assimilation across national boundaries and his final statement on form, voice, and transcendent energy. Celebrating the glory of the American West and the unmatched passion of the Italian operas, Whitman asserts that

> [. . .] not to the city's fresco'd rooms, not to the audience of the
>   opera house,
> Sounds, echoes, wandering strains, as really here at home,
> *Sonnambula's* innocent love, trios with *Norma's* anguish,
> And thy ecstatic chorus *Poliuto*;

> Ray'd in the limpid yellow slanting sundown,
> Music, Italian music in Dakota. (lines 7–12)

Examples of the art form that initially seemed so artificial and foreign to Whitman share the same space with the untamed wilderness of America's western landscape. Like many of his contemporaries, Whitman originally viewed Italian opera with skepticism. His early words of praise were reserved for more homespun melodies and "non-technical singing performances" (Whitman, *Complete* 7: 52) like those of the Hutchinson band. In "Music that Is Music," (*Brooklyn Daily Eagle*, December 4, 1846), Whitman claims that "the music of feeling—heart music as distinguished from art music—is well exemplified in such singing as the Hutchinsons' and several other bands of American vocalists," while Italian opera is a "stale, second hand, foreign method" (*Gathering* 347–48). But eventually, Whitman embraced Italian opera as the suitable metaphor for an American musical expression that would be available to everyone—not just those gathered under the gaslights of the opera house. In "Italian Music in Dakota," Whitman asserted that opera belongs not only in the glamorous and exclusive halls of the opera houses but also in the "endless wilds, / In dulcet streams" the "gnarled realm" of the American Dakotas (lines 2–3, 13). In his earlier prose writings, Whitman adamantly called for an "American Opera. When a song is sung the accompaniment to be by only one instrument or two instruments the rest silent—the vocal performer to make far more of his song, or solo part, by by-play, attitudes, expression, movements, &c. than is at all made by the Italian opera singers—The American opera to be far more simple, and give far more scope to the persons enacting the characters" (qtd. in Furness 201–2). As his exposure to opera expanded, Whitman's anxieties about a foreign art form fell away; he embraced the Italian opera and its ability to "express the simplest sounds properly" (*New York* 22).

Through his poetry and prose, he invites all Americans, regardless of class or geography, to enter into the operatic world with him. The opening lines of "The Opera," written for *Life Illustrated*, issue Whitman's call:

> We invite you to spend an evening with us at the opera, and

> listen to the music, and look at the place and people. You there, away so far from New York, perhaps in Ohio, or Wisconsin, or up toward Canada, or away northeast or southeast, you need not travel hither; you can stop home and do your day's work, and at candle-light come into your own house and wash and put on some clean clothes, no matter how coarse, and then eat your supper, and sit down at the table or by the fire, and we will bring the opera to you—even the Italian opera—in full bloom. (*New York* 18)

Less interested in relating the literal words of the libretto, he strives to translate the sounds of the music for his audience. Whitman's pen transforms the tones that seem unintelligible to many into articulate thoughts and emotions, transcending the boundaries between audible and written speech. He describes his recognition of these voices in "That Music Always Round Me," published in the 1860 edition of *Leaves of Grass:*

> That music always round me, unceasing, unbeginning, yet long untaught I did not hear,
> But now the chorus I hear and am elated,
> A tenor, strong, ascending with power and health, with glad notes of daybreak I hear,
> A soprano at intervals sailing buoyantly over the tops of immense waves,
> A transparent base shuddering lusciously under and through the universe,
> The triumphant tutti, the funeral wailings with sweet flutes and violins, all these I fill myself with,
> I hear not the volumes of sound merely, I am moved by the exquisite meanings,
> I listen to the different voices winding in and out, striving, contending with fiery vehemence to excel each other in emotion;
> I do not think the performers know themselves—but now I think I begin to know them. (lines 1–9)

He acknowledges that he remained "long untaught" (line 1), unable to hear the voices of the tenor and soprano, referring to those days when he viewed opera merely as an artificial and foreign form. After learning to listen, however, Whitman experiences the physical transformation of the music "fill[ing] [him]self" (line 6) with the "volumes of sound" (line 7). For many listeners, the operatic experience ends with the reception of sound and the bodily response it provokes. Whitman, however, is "moved by the exquisite meanings" (line 7), and he claims to "know" (9) the performers and the messages they express through the "different voices winding in and out, striving, contending with fiery vehemence to excel each other in emotion" (line 8). Through the process of translating, Whitman embodies the poetic identity, transcending the limits of written speech. In his use of opera, Whitman recovers the audible voice of the bard. By offering his translations to every reader, Whitman democratizes opera, offering its sounds, emotions, and messages to all who will listen.

2

DIVIDED ATTENTION

The Opera House in Poe and Alcott

While the American Gothic tale certainly owes much to its European predecessors, it often replaced the highly supernatural events of its precursors with the psychological. The eighteenth-century novels of Charles Brockden Brown (one of the first and most influential practitioners of American Gothicism) "embody Gothic horrors, but those horrors prove to have bases in human psychology rather than in the presumed supernatural horrors" (Fisher 77). Influenced by Brown, Edgar Allan Poe "divined how he could manipulate conventions of Gothicism to create fine psychological fiction" (Fisher 84). As Poe's readers and critics readily acknowledge, his works are devoted to mining the interior spaces of his characters' minds. Not surprisingly, Poe discovered in the opera house an ideal setting for such an exploration. "Given its hybridity and its popularity," suggest Avril Horner and Sue Zlosnik, "it is perhaps no coincidence that the rise of the Gothic novel is roughly contemporary not only with the birth of melodrama but also with the rise of the circus and of opera as popular entertainment" (6). Poe relished the versatility of the Gothic tale, and he recognized similar potential in opera. In "The Spectacles," Poe exploits the comic potential of Gothic, producing humor rather than horror. Replacing the haunted castle, the opera house in "The Spectacles" provides the ideal Gothic space for considering the interiority of the human mind (its perceptions and deceptions) and the exteriority of appearance and convention (operatic and social).

Poe's extended tenure as a journalist made him familiar with the stars, composers, compositions, and venues of opera in America, but unlike Whitman, he left little evidence of his exposure to opera in journal entries or letters. The editorials from his New York years suggest that Poe regularly attended the opera as a reviewer. His immersion in opera, however, predates his arrival at New York's *Mirror* or *Broadway.* "The Spectacles" first appears in the *Dollar Newspaper* on March 27, 1844. This short story, written before his New York experience, demonstrates that Poe already possessed an operatic sensibility and a sophisticated knowledge of the genre, enabling him to create rich layers of narrative irony. On a surface level, the story displays an awareness of the contemporary opera scene with references to the acclaimed soprano Malibran and to San Carlo, a famous opera venue. More tellingly, Poe describes vocal technique as though he possessed an intimate knowledge of the art: "Her lower tones were miraculous. Her voice embraced three complete octaves, extending from the contralto D to the D upper soprano, and, though sufficiently powerful to have filled the San Carlos [*sic*], executed, with the minutest precision, every difficulty of vocal composition—ascending and descending scales, cadences, or *fioriture*" (Harrison 5: 197). He also exhibits a familiarity with specific operas and composers, Rossini's *Otello* and Bellini's *La Sonnambula.* Such extensive use of operatic allusion would require more than a passing familiarity with the genre.

In April 1844, Poe moved to New York where he accepted a job with the *Evening Mirror.* One of the *Mirror*'s editors, George Pope Morris, referred to the paper as "the organ of the 'upper ten thousand,' reflecting his intention of speaking to and for the social world," relates Kenneth Silverman. Those in Morris's targeted audience were the ones that Poe "regarded sourly as 'the frivolous and fashionable' " (Silverman 225). While the job at the *Mirror* did not offer Poe the type of writing opportunities he valued, it did introduce him to the world of New York's upper crust and its cultural entertainments. The journal's advertisements described its orientation this way: "The New Mirror, or Literature, Amusement, and Instruction: Containing Original Papers; Tales of Romance; Sketches of Society, Manners, and Every-day Life; Domestic and Foreign Correspondence; Wit and Humour; Fashion and Gossip; the Fine Arts, and Literary, Musical, and Dramatic Criticism." Although Poe considered himself a literary reviewer, not a musical critic, his employment at the *Mirror* opened the city's musical events, including operas, to him.

In "Why Have the New Yorkers No Review," published in the *Mirror,* Poe issued a call for a literary magazine worthy of the intellectual community in New York, and even while working at the *Mirror,* he contributed pieces to a new weekly, the *Broadway Journal.* In the early months of 1845, he joined the editorial staff of the *Broadway Journal.* The February 22 edition announced that, "hereafter, Edgar A. Poe and Henry C. Watson, will be associated with the Editorial department of our Journal" (*Broadway Journal* 127). While this announcement claims that Watson will oversee the articles about music, the "Musical Criticism" column of the same edition directly criticizes Poe's former employer. "In answer to the editor of the *Mirror,*" responded the *Journal,* "we must reiterate what we have before said, that his musical opinions are of no value; they would not even serve as make weight to a doubting mind." The diatribe continues: "His criticisms, as criticisms, are without meaning: being a mere string of strained similes, far-fetched images, irrelevant rhapsodies, which, though expressed by a strange mixture of quaintness and bombast, flippancy and earnestness, bear no internal evidence that they spring either from a knowledge or a love of the subject in discussion." The writer calls the *Mirror*'s editor an "Operatic Puffer" who "has endeavored to foster a false standard of taste, by exalting (O Power of imagination!) merely good talent into superior genius; he has encouraged negligence and slovenliness in every department, by indiscriminate commendation" ("Musical Criticism" 124). In contrast, the *Broadway Journal* would "raise the Art by preserving it and its professors in a course of integrity" (124). Even though the weekly identified the head of its musical department as another editor, three men—C. F. Briggs, Edgar A. Poe, and Henry C. Watson—would actually contribute reviews. By July 12, 1845, only Poe and Watson remained as editors of the journal, so both men were needed to cover the numerous musical and theatrical events occurring in the city. In October of the same year, Poe assumed the position of sole editor and proprietor. Unfortunately, the musical reviews were not signed, but Poe likely penned many of them.

As the reviews demonstrate, the editors of the *Broadway* acted as strong advocates for opera. They covered performances delivered at the Park, Niblo's Garden, Castle Garden, and Palmo's. These reviewers recognized the importance of the genre both as an art form and as a cultural event. The March 1845 editions of the journal include speculation about the building of a new opera house—presumably the Astor Place Opera House, which would eventually open in November 1848. The March 8 edition includes this bit: "They talk of building an Opera-house up town!! We maintain that this is news, for many people will naturally believe that after so much talk, something is doing. But we inform them, *that they talk*" ("Home News" 158). Two weeks later, the "Musical Items" section states, "We hear nothing of the new opera house; nor of the short season at Palmo's with the Italians now in this city; nor of the proposed managerial speculation of Signor De Begnis" (190).

Significantly, during his tenure as editor at the *Broadway,* Poe republished "The Spectacles" in the November 22, 1845, edition. Called the "most absurd of the Grotesques" (400) by one of Poe's many biographers, Kenneth Silverman, "The Spectacles" uses opera to explore the theme of vision and vanity. With the act of perception so unstable in the story, the grotesquery of delusion emerges. The central conflict of the tale occurs in the opera house, an ideal setting for a consideration of perception and deception. In "Edgar Allan Poe: The Sublime and the Grotesque," Frederick L. Burwick observes that often Poe "sets his tale in a descriptive space that is interchangeably physical and mental" (71). The dual suggestions of setting underscore the significance of perception in Poe's stories, particularly in "The Spectacles." As Burwick's title suggests, Poe's tale focuses on "how the phenomena are apprehended"; the conclusion considers the "dislocation/relocation" of the perceptual process (71). From the opening lines of the tale, Poe turns the reader's attention to vision:

> Many years ago, it was the fashion to ridicule the idea of "love at first sight"; but those who think, not less than those who feel deeply, have always advocated its existence. Modern discoveries, indeed, in what may be termed ethical magnetism or magneto-aesthetics, render it probable that the most natural,

> and, consequently, the truest and most intense of the human affections are those which arise in the heart as if by electric sympathy—in a word, that the brightest and most enduring of the psychal fetters are those which are riveted by a glance. (Harrison 5: 177)

That glance determines the course of the story's central conflict and ultimate resolution. To complicate matters, Poe gives the story's narrator, Napoleon Bonaparte Simpson—a man who is by "no means deficient" in "personal endowments"—one defect: eyes that are "weak to a very inconvenient degree" (178). Simpson explains that "the weakness, itself, however, has always much annoyed me, and I have resorted to every remedy—short of wearing glasses" (178–79). An even greater vulnerability than the physical limitation, however, is the vanity that prevents him from seeking corrective measures. "Being youthful and good-looking," Simpson admits, "I naturally dislike these [glasses], and have resolutely refused to employ them." He finds the remedy to his weakness so distasteful that he claims to "know nothing, indeed, which so disfigures the countenance of a young person, or so impresses every feature with an air of demureness, if not altogether of sanctimoniousness and of age. An eye-glass, on the other hand, has a savor of downright foppery and affectation" (179).

Claiming that these personal details are "of little importance" (179), the narrator goes on to relate his experiences at the opera house, identified as the P___ Theatre, perhaps a reference to New York's Park Theatre, the location of the first performance of grand opera in that city. "It was an opera night,"[1] Simpson recalls, "and the bills presented a very rare attraction, so that the house was excessively crowded" (179). The performance in the opera house is not limited to the one offered on the stage. While his companion "gave his undivided attention to the stage," Simpson "amused [himself] by observing the audience [. . .]" (179). The young man finds his gaze "arrested and riveted by a figure in one of the private boxes [. . .]" (179). Neglecting the prima donna on stage, Simpson "gazed at this queenly apparition for at least half an hour," having "felt the full force and truth of all that has been said or sung concerning 'love at first sight' " (180–81).

Judith Saunders notes that Poe, like Emerson, believed that "the poet is far more likely than the scientist to recognize the possibility and the importance of changing perspective. He is actively experimental, even playful, in his efforts to apprehend the world" (69). As numerous Poe scholars have observed, Poe's interest in vision and perception transcends the genre or mode of his writing. In his short stories and poems, in his detective stories, his darker tales, and his comedies, Poe considers the question of human perception.[2] Although neither the reader nor the narrator is aware of it at the opening of "The Spectacles," the vision that Simpson offers does not reflect reality. In this example of American Gothic, the "terrors" that are experienced by Poe's characters "come from faulty perception. They either perceive what is not objectively present or they misinterpret even the commonplace elements of the everyday world, transforming them into objects of terror" (Ringe 25). "Susceptible to the enhancements of memory and the disfigurations of madness," beauty resides "in the mind of the beholder, [. . .] subject to the mind's conditions of instability and change" (Burwick 77). Poe limits the physical and the psychic vision of the narrator. Controlled by his weak eyesight, Simpson's perceptions are unstable. "As one emotion or another sways that perception," observes Burwick, "the beautiful may be heightened by terror into the sublime, distorted into the grotesque, ornamentally exaggerated into the arabesque" (91). By using opera, Poe creates a setting ruled simultaneously by a grotesque and an arabesque reality.

Because the stage imitates reality, it offers a refracted vision. The singer-actors embody their roles, wearing makeup and costumes that make them believable to an observer. Fundamentally, however, they remain unchanged. Like Madame Lalande, the opera singers engage in the art of disguise behind wigs and wardrobe. All these devices, however, fail to erase the wrinkled skin, feeble voice, and toothless gums of an eighty-two-year-old woman. Similarly, on the stage the regal robes fail to transform the diva completely into royalty. Embracing such artifice, Poe utilizes the "comic turn": "the deliberate exploitation of the stylized theatricality of the Gothic; a concern with the artificial, [. . .] a ludic quality that involves obsession with fakery. Even as it creates its effects of terror and horror and claims authenticity, it reveals its mechanisms" (Horner and Zlosnik 166). The ideal world created in the theater will not withstand the final curtain call. When that veil between the performed reality and the audience falls, the illusion is destroyed. Unlike other forms of drama, however, opera transcends the limitation of theatrics. Instead of dialogue alone, opera also relies upon the power of music to communicate its ideas. Poe claimed that "music, when combined with a pleasurable idea," as in opera, "is poetry" (Harrison 7: xliii). In the same letter, he describes the "indefinite" pleasure of listening to music, allowing the listener to transcend the limitations of reality and embrace an ideality: an arabesque reality. Aware of the power of the opera's music—its voice—Poe includes in his tale not only an opera on stage but also a parlor performance of operatic numbers.

In "The Spectacles," the narrator finds himself in a peculiar position. His auditory receptors are unmarred, but his vision is deficient. Ironically, the assumptions that he makes based on both of these senses are equally false. Because opera depends upon both the visual and auditory senses to achieve its ends, it offers Poe an ideal mode for depicting a narrator whose flaw, apparently physical, is actually rooted in his character. By placing the action at the opera house, Poe establishes a parallel within his narrative. As a mixed genre, opera incorporates elements of drama, music, and dance into a single performance. The audience must devote its eyes and ears to the action onstage in order to experience fully the production. From the opening lines of the story, Simpson's attention is divided, dooming the accuracy of his perceptions. These inaccuracies are first revealed in the opera house. Focusing on the occupants of the box seats rather than the performance unfolding onstage, Simpson gazes at "grace personified, incarnate, the *beau idéal* of my wildest and most enthusiastic visions" (Harrison 5: 180). In addition to admiring the beauty of the woman in the box, Simpson observes the jewels ornamenting her attire, suggesting the "wealth and fastidious taste of the wearer" (180). As Poe observed in "The Philosophy of Furniture," "We [Americans] have not aristocracy of blood, and having therefore as a natural, and indeed as an inevitable thing, fashioned for ourselves an aristocracy of dollars, the display of wealth has here to take the place and perform the office of the heraldic display in monarchical countries" (Harrison 14: 101). The extravagance and elegance of the box holders' habiliments invited the public to project other qualities—like royalty—onto these representatives of America's elite.

As the reviews found in Poe's journals discuss, the opera provided a perfect venue for the display of wealth. Taste, wealth, and social standing were determined in large measure by the "display of dress and fashion" ("Operas and Concerts" 59). This deceptive display allowed the wealthy to masquerade as royalty and aristocracy. In the January 25, 1845, installment, the editors of the *Broadway* asserted that they "greatly distrust this violent and sudden excitement about the Italian opera. It is not the expression of a discriminating and healthy public appreciation, but it is rather the fussy clamor of a set or clique, with no further end in view than the passing away of idle hours, combined with affected display of dress and fashion" (59). The editors associate Italian opera with the "Upper Ten Thousand" of New York's wealthy elite, while the English Opera's "efforts are more beneficial to the mass" (59). Although Italian opera had been appearing in New York since its debut there in 1825, the journalists reviewing it (including those at the *Broadway Journal*) remained skeptical of its influence, perhaps out of a keen distaste for the audience that patronized it.

Poe demonstrates his distrust of the privileged class by introducing Simpson as a man willing to change his name in order to inherit a fortune and ascend the ranks of the wealthy. Comically, in Poe's story a French woman, with a legitimate pedigree, who defies the customs and conventions of America's elite represents the true aristocracy. Not only does Madame Lalande lift her opera glass to gaze at Simpson despite the disapproving looks, she also engineers a plot of deceit against her misguided admirer. By turning the expectations of the reader upside down, Poe enhances the comedic element of his grotesque tale.

In the opening pages of the story, Simpson notes that "the stern decrees of Fashion had, of late, imperatively prohibited the use of the opera-glass, in a case such as this [staring at a woman in the audience], even had [he] been so fortunate as to have one with [him]" (Harrison 5: 182). He must steal glances only "when [he] [thinks] the audience [is] fully engaged with the opera" (186). Exerting his male gaze, Simpson consumes the object of his affection. The narrator explains that he "feasted [his] eyes" on Madame Lalande, consuming her in the intensity of [his] gaze" (184). The object of his gaze, in turn, violates the convention of acceptable behavior. As Simpson tells us, "she actually took from her girdle a double eye-glass—elevated it—adjusted it—and then regarded me through it, intently and deliberately, for the space of several minutes" (184). Disregarding the critical eyes of the audience, she studies Simpson. With Madame Lalande's violation of propriety, Poe reverses the reader's assumptions about power and gender in the story. "In a world ordered by sexual imbalance, pleasure in looking has been split between active/male and passive/female," observes Laura Mulvey. "The determining male gaze projects its fantasy onto the female figure, which is styled accordingly," Mulvey explains. "In their traditional exhibitionist role women are simultaneously looked at and displayed, with their appearance coded for strong visual and erotic impact so that they can be said to connote *to-be-looked-at-ness*. Woman displayed as sexual object is the *leitmotif* of erotic spectacle [. . .]" (19). As his narrator's detailed descriptions of Madame Lalande's jewels and attire demonstrate, Poe recognized the dual display of wealth and women occurring in the opera boxes. However, he reverses the roles of spectator and object. By empowering Madame Lalande as a gazer, the "binary lines of male/female, gazer/object, dominant/submissive are at least temporarily destabilized" (Johnson 44). Gazing at her subject "with so much quietude—so much *nonchalance*—so much repose—with so evident an air of the highest breeding" (Harrison 5: 184), Madame Lalande reinvigorates the passive female with power and dignity.

Even as her actions "gave rise to an indefinite movement, or *buzz*, among the audience" (Harrison 5: 185), Madame Lalande exudes confidence and authority. In *Discipline and Punish: The Birth of the Prison*, Michel Foucault charts the dynamics of power in Western culture. According to him, as the eighteenth century turned into the nineteenth, Western society moved from a system of spectacle (illustrated by public punishments such as torturing, hanging, burning, etc.) to a system of surveillance (exemplified by Bentham's Panopticon, an invention that imprisoned a captive under the constant and watchful gaze of his keepers—without enabling the prisoner to see his guards). In his discussion of Bentham's Panopticon, Foucault considers the roles of vision and the gaze in establishing the modern system of power. Producing a state of "conscious and permanent visibility that assures the automatic functioning of power," the Panopticon provided power that was "visible" yet still "unverifiable" (201). Even though the subject of the Panopticon's gaze could not see his observer, he knew that he constantly remained under surveillance. The opera house provides a similar opportunity for a visible yet unverifiable power. While those seated in the box seats, like Madame Lalande, are presumably engrossed in the performance occurring onstage, they simultaneously remain surrounded by the gazes and glances of fellow audience members. Because the "all-powerful cultural gaze" is "implicitly male" (Johnson 40), the exchange of glances between Simpson and Madame Lalande exhibits a silent dialogue about power and sexuality. By replacing the passive female with an active gazer, Poe subverts the cultural norm.

By empowering Madame Lalande, Poe diminishes Simpson's credibility, thereby enhancing the comedic element of the story. Because the dominant culture accepted what Linda Nochlin describes as "assumptions about women's weakness and passivity; her sexual availability for men's needs; her defining domestic and nurturing function; her identity with the realm of nature; her existence as object rather than creator of art" (2), Madame Lalande's behavior is even more radical. Not only does she defy propriety by lifting her opera glasses and submitting a man to her gaze, she concocts and implements a plot of deception with the help of Simpson's friend Talbot. Refusing to remain a passive victim of a man's consuming gaze, Madame Lalande reverses the roles. At the conclusion of the story, the narrator attributes his reprimanding to his "imprudence" in "making open love, in a theatre, to an old woman unknown" (Harrison 5: 208), not to his inability to admit his own limitations. Even with perfect vision, however, the narrator would have been led astray by his perception.

Not only does Simpson's vision deceive him, but his ears also lead his perceptions astray. After his initial encounter with Madame Lalande at the opera, Simpson pursues the object of his affection, making his initial overture by letter. Too impatient to wait for a proper introduction, Simpson confronts the lady as she promenades outside her home. During this exchange, she invites him into her home for a "little musical levee" (195). "I can promise you, too, some good singing," Madame explains to Simpson; "We French are not nearly so punctilious as you Americans, and I shall have no difficulty in smuggling you in, in the character of an old acquaintance" (196). The evening's entertainment offers singing that Simpson claims he "had never heard excelled in any private circle out of Vienna" (196). "At length, upon a peremptory call for 'Madame Lalande,' she arose at once, without affectation or demur, from the *chaise longue* upon which she had sate by my side," he explains. Madame Lalande, "accompanied by one or two gentlemen and her female friend of the opera, repaired to the piano in the main drawing-room" (196). As Simpson explains in the final pages of the story, "When 'Madame Lalande' was called upon to sing, the younger lady (Madame Stéphanie Lalande) was intended" (208). Because he was "deprived of the pleasure of seeing, although not of hearing" (197) Madame Lalande where he was sitting during the concert, Simpson mistakenly believes he is listening to the object of his desire. Instead, the lovely, young voice belongs to her granddaughter. He describes what he hears in Madame Lalande's drawing room with great detail:

> It is beyond the reach of art to endow either air or recitative with more impassioned *expression* than was hers. Her utterance of the romance in Otello—the tone with which she gave the words "*Sul mio sasso,*" in the Capuletti—is ringing in my memory yet. Her lower tones were absolutely miraculous. Her voice embraced three complete octaves, extending from the contralto D to the D upper soprano, and, though sufficiently powerful to have filled the San Carlos, executed, with the minutest precision, every difficulty of vocal composition—ascending and descending scales, cadences, or *fioriture.* In the finale of the Sonnambula, she brought about a most remarkable effect at the words—
>
> Ah! non guinge uman pensiero
> Al contento ond 'io son piena.
>
> Here, in imitation of Malibran, she modified the original phrase of Bellini, so as to let her voice descend to the tenor G,

> when, by a rapid transition, she struck the G above the treble stave, springing over an interval of two octaves. (197)

Poe draws upon an impressive knowledge of voice types, vocal ranges, librettos, and opera performers in weaving his web of illusion. As other opera aficionados would recognize, Poe names his story's heroine, Madame Lalande, for one of Madame Malibran's real-life opera rivals. In a letter included in *Memoirs and Letters of Madame Malibran* (1840), Malibran, writing to an intimate friend, offers an unflattering account of her rival's debut. Malibran claims that "Madame Lalande sang it without spirit, and consequently produced no effect," leading to the general opinion that "she was very mediocre" (qtd. in Merlin, 122).

Not surprisingly, Poe chooses for the drawing room concert excerpts from operas that revolve around misperceptions and deceptions. In Rossini's *Otello* and Bellini's *La Sonnambula*, the heroines are accused of being unfaithful to their lovers—Otello and Elvino—because of misplaced tokens of affection—a handkerchief and a veil. Though the charges against Desdemona and Amina are false, the women appear guilty when they are unable to explain how they lost the handkerchief and the veil. In fact, the lines from Amina's aria that Poe includes in the text, translated as "Oh, recall not one earthly sorrow, / With the blisses of heav'n around us," are followed by an explanation of the culprit in this lover's quarrel: faulty perception. Amina sings, "An illusion it was that bound us, / Thou, Elvino, art true to love" (*La Sonnambula* 193–94). Just as things are not what they seem in these plots, Poe's unsuspecting lover fails to read his own false perceptions. While Simpson's ears accurately analyze the characteristics of the voice he hears, he fails to identify its source correctly. He does, however, express some doubt about the ability of Madame Lalande to produce "these miracles of vocal execution" (Harrison 5: 197–98). He explains that he was "most unfeignedly surprised" to hear those sounds from the object of his admiration because "a certain feebleness, or rather a certain tremulous indecision of voice in ordinary conversation, had prepared me to anticipate that, in singing, she would not acquit herself with any remarkable ability" (198). As the reader learns, the quiver in Madame Lalande's voice indicates her advanced age.

With comedic irony, the narrator falls victim to his own misconceptions and misperceptions. Rewriting the male gaze, Poe disables the consumptive power of Simpson's eyes and restores the empowering role to the subject of his gaze, Madame Lalande. When she defies social propriety and convention by openly returning his gaze, she shifts the focus. Instead of allowing herself to be objectified, she controls the field of vision. Rather than openly deceiving Simpson, she merely plays to his preconceived notions about her identity. Like the diva onstage, Lalande does not have to conform to reality. As the object of Simpson's affections, she creates the illusion that he expects. Because he perceives the world through "half-closed eyes,"[3] Simpson's reality is blurred by both his literal and his figurative inability to see clearly. His failing vision prevents him from seeing the aged woman hidden beneath the "pearl-powder, of rouge, of false hair, false teeth, and false *tournure,* as well as of the skilful modistes of Paris" (206). When the Madame Lalande of Simpson's dreams is unveiled as Madame Eugénie Lalande—his own great, great grandmother—the grotesque and the arabesque elements of Poe's tale collide. The deception occurring in the story constitutes the grotesque. Only when Simpson's sense of reality is sharpened by the use of an eyeglass, does he discover the path to the ideality he originally pursued: Madame Stéphanie Lalande. Describing Poe's technique, Ketterer explains that "to see truly the deceptive nature of reality is to see simultaneously the actuality. In a sense, then, the arabesque concept subsumes the grotesque. To see human reality as grotesque is to intuit simultaneously intimations of an arabesque reality" (37). In "The Spectacles," Poe reveals his interest in the grotesque not only by exposing deception but also by considering the source of Simpson's errant judgments.

While Poe scholars looking to characterize his work as Gothic rarely discuss "The Spectacles," the story includes many of the elements that typically define that genre. "Gothic plots tend to be organized around anxieties and uncertainties generated by those examples of language that mark the intersections of 'nature' and 'culture': wedding vows, wills, and the laws regulating the family, such as the principles of 'legitimate' succession and inheritance," notes Anne Williams. "Problems with such codes often (especially in early Gothic) lead the characters to confront the broader surrounding context of 'natural' law, particularly the incest taboo" (68). Merging the comic with the Gothic, Poe begins his story with a narrator who defies his own identity by changing his name in order to receive a substantial inheritance from a distant male relative. The narrator explains that his "name, at present, is a very usual and rather plebian one—Simpson." He uses the term "at present" because he only "legislatively adopted this surname within the last year" when the "bequest was conditioned upon [his] taking the name of the testator" (Harrison 5: 177), Adolphus Simpson, Esq. Rejecting his "true patronym, Froissart" (178), Simpson denies the natural law of family succession.

Ironically, at the story's conclusion, the object of his skewed perceptions, Madame Eugénie Lalande, explains that she came to America "for the purpose of making [Simpson] her heir" (207). In broken English, illustrative of the anxieties and uncertainties of language that Anne Williams refers to, Madame Lalande tells Simpson that "my daughter's daughter, Mademoiselle Voissart, she marry von Monsieur Croissart, and, den agin, my daughter's grande daughter, Mademoiselle Croissart, she marry von Monsieur Froissart" (205). She concludes this brief genealogy by asserting that "Monsieur Froissart, he vas von *ver* big vat you call fool—he vas von *ver* great big donce like yourself—for he lef *la belle France* for come to dis stupide Amérique—and ven he get here he vent and ave von *ver* stupide, von *ver, ver* stupide sonn [. . .]." Building to a crescendo of comic irony, Madame concludes by revealing that "he is name de Napoléon Bonaparte Froissart" (205). By forsaking his real name, Simpson (or, Froissart) thwarts the natural course of familial lineage and succession. To further entrench the story in this Gothic anxiety about meaning, Poe invokes the incest taboo by including a wedding, albeit fake, between a great, great grandmother and her unsuspecting descendant. The delight of the reader differs greatly from Simpson's "horrific" and "hideous" astonishment, marked by "terror" and "rage" (203–4). The self-deceiver has been deceived again.

In "The Rival Prima Donnas," Louisa May Alcott also relies upon the opera box to explore the divided attention of performers and audience. From the opening lines, the narrator draws the reader's focus to the public display of women in the opera house. "The opera house was filling fast with a gay and brilliant audience, empty boxes grew bright with lovely women, jewels sparkled, plumes waved, and fans began to move" (Alcott 37). The audience participates in a consumptive spectacle of beauty, fashion, and wealth. The display's power is heightened when the conversation turns to the empty box seat of Beatrice, the "pride and favorite [soprano] of the public" (37). One of Alcott's earliest stories, "The Rival Prima Donnas" demonstrates her interest in the deep divide between the public and private spheres and the gendered roles that dominated the distinctions within those spheres. Writing under the pseudonym Flora Fairfield, Alcott earned ten dollars for the story, which appeared in the November 11, 1854, edition of Boston's *Saturday Evening Gazette.*[4] Some critics read the story as a fictionalized account of the real-life duel between Henrietta Sontag and Marietta Alboni, reigning divas of the nineteenth-century stage. Yet, Alcott goes beyond these models in crafting the story. Through multilayered operatic allusions, Alcott instructs her audience on how to resolve the conflicting readings of the story. The first interpretation, supported by the postlude, assumes that the heroine, Beatrice, commits a murder because of her madness. An alternative reading interprets Beatrice as a cold-blooded and cruel murderess. The operatic allusions, however, provide a clarifying synthesis for these two interpretations. Alcott's fictional narrative explores the fate of the nineteenth-century diva, the embodiment of the female artist's voice.

Although there are no biographical details in Alcott's story to confirm that Alboni and Sontag served as her sources, their historical contemporaneity to the composition of Alcott's story suggests a connection. Published in the same year that the highly acclaimed German soprano Sontag died, Alcott's story no doubt reminded readers of the real life rivalry between Sontag and Marietta Alboni, an Italian contralto. Alboni came to New York in 1852, and her influence on Walt Whitman was well documented in his prose writings. As opera historian John Dizikes explains, "In the fall of 1852 Alboni and Sontag opposed each other in direct concert-hall rivalry, often singing in the same cities at the same time" (143). Most critics seemed to agree that Alboni possessed the superior voice, but Sontag "personified the diva as great lady, great beyond her musical gifts," appearing in "magnificent gowns that cost fabulous sums" and wearing "glittering diamond necklaces and gold bracelets" (143–44). The rivalry that began in the concert hall extended to the opera stage in the winter of 1853. On many nights, the two divas not only sang in rival opera houses but also often performed the very same opera!

In *Queens of Song*, Ellen Clayton describes Alboni's voice:

> Her voice was a superb contralto, yet embracing almost three octaves, from E flat to C sharp: its tones were rich, full, sonorous, mellow, liquid; in truth, the vocabulary of epithets might be exhausted in a vain endeavor to convey an idea of its beauty. Its quality throughout was equally pure, beautiful, flexible, and sympathetic. Her articulation was clear; her notes came, even in the most difficult and rapid passages with the fluency and precision of a well-played instrument. The purity of her intonation was absolutely faultless; the rapidity and certainty of her execution no one can imagine who has not heard her. Her style and method were models of perfection, her taste was refined, her skill consummate. (441)

A role that Alboni performed in America was the title part in Bellini's *Norma*. Composed for a coloratura soprano, the role was not suited to Alboni's voice and had to be transposed down for her. Richard Grant White, who heard the two performances that Alboni delivered, described her singing in this way: "*Norma*-ly, it [Alboni attempting this role] was open to objection." He speculated that she "must have brooded over the part until it took complete possession of her [. . .]. In its own way it was a very great performance" (qtd. in Dizikes 144). Embodying one of the greatest tragic roles in opera, Alboni conquered a part many thought she could never undertake.

Having married Carlo de Rossi, a nobleman and diplomat at the court of King Carlo Felice of Sardinia, Sontag came to America a countess, though a recently impoverished one. Her social position stirred interest in the American public, and her visit was also publicized by Le Grand Smith, a former employee of P. T. Barnum (who had promoted Jenny Lind's American tour). Describing Sontag's voice, Clayton notes, "Henrietta's voice was a pure soprano, reaching perhaps from A or B to D in alt, and, though uniform in its quality, it was a little reedy in the lower notes, but its flexibility was marvelous: in the high octave, from F to C in alt, her notes rang out like the tones of a silver bell. The clearness of her notes, the precision of her intonation, the fertility of her invention, and the facility of her execution, were displayed in brilliant flights and lavish fioriture; her rare flexibility being a natural gift, cultivated by taste and incessant study" (300). According to Dizikes, Sontag's "chief strength was that she had a clearer sense, which she imparted to some extent to her colleagues, of the opera as a whole." Despite this understanding, however, "she lacked dramatic power" (144).

Unlike Alcott's Beatrice, neither Alboni nor Sontag responded to their rivalry with a violent act of revenge, but each artist certainly knew the cost of losing the battle waged between them. In Clayton's study of the "celebrated female vocalists who have performed on the lyric stage," she records many of "those vindictive contests of which musical history has so many instances" (306). She discusses the competitive relationship between Sontag and Malibran (the diva to whom Poe referred in "The Spectacles") and the role spectators played in promoting the contest. "The rivalry between Malibran and Sontag now broke out afresh with redoubled vehemence, and reached such a height that they would not even meet in the same salon," notes Clayton. "The partisans of each as it always happens, contributed to give to this rivalry an aspect of vindictiveness, and on the stage, when they sang in the same opera, their jealously was scareely [*sic*] disguised" (306).

Employing the Sontag-Malibran rivalry, Alcott added another dimension to the tension between the domestic and the public sphere, between artistic freedom and cultural expectations, between authority and submission. Often it was necessary for the female artist to sacrifice domestic tranquility for success. The two singers in "The Rival Prima Donnas" vie not only for the affections of the same audience but also for the same lover, the painter Claude. Alcott's story creates a clear tension between the public and the private sphere. Teresa, the diva who attempts to have it all—success on the opera stage and in a love relationship—dies at the hands of her rival. Alcott remains unable to imagine—even creatively—a workable melding of the private and public spheres.

Longing to inhabit the private sphere, Beatrice abandons her life as a performer to accept Claude's proposal of marriage. On the night she willingly passes the accolades of her adoring audience to her would-be rival, Theresa, the curtains of Beatrice's box seat are flung open. Beatrice, "radiant in beauty," refocuses the audience's gaze toward her rival, down on the stage, "cast[ing] the flowers from her own bosom" (39) at Theresa's feet. In an ardent speech to Claude she elevates the domestic sphere above the public one:

> Have I not tried the world and found its flattering homage false? Have I not sought for happiness in wealth and fame and sought in vain until I found it in your love? What then do I leave but all I am most weary of? And what do I gain but all I prize and cherish most on earth? The painter's home I will make beautiful with the useless wealth I have won, and the painter's heart I will make happy by all the blessings a woman's love can give! Then do not fear for me. What can I lose in leaving a careless world for a husband and a home? (39)

In contrast, Beatrice's rival—Theresa—seeks her joy in the "fame and wealth I will soon win" (42). Rather than seeking the refuge of the private sphere, Theresa urges Beatrice's lover Claude to join her in reveling in the accolades of the public realm. Fleeing a life of poverty, isolation, and friendlessness, Theresa craves the garlands and bouquets that symbolize the public's affection for her. Reviews of actual opera performances, like the following from the *New York Times*, recorded the various floral tokens of appreciation given to singers: "There was a prolific display of floral tributes to Mme. Gerster, including a laurel lyre, a basket of flowers, a crown surmounting a basket of roses and a floral wreath, three bouquets, one crown of laurel, and one cross of roses and lilies" ("A Crowd at the Academy"). Flowers tossed upon the stage during a performance demonstrated the audience's appreciation for an outstanding performance, but they also posed a danger to the performer. As she stood accepting the outpouring of admiration from her audience, the diva also placed herself in a precarious position—the unintentional target of these forcefully flung tokens of affection. Alcott recognizes this possibility and uses it to create a dark ending for her story.

Ironically, Beatrice chooses a token of admiration as her weapon of choice. After realizing that Theresa is now a rival in love, as she had earlier been in art, Beatrice disguises her hatred as admiration: "Shall I not rather weave them (roses) into a garland for the lovely Theresa, for whom they are fitter ornaments than for me? I will crown her with roses, that the world may see I neither fear nor envy her. Think not that I slight your gift, Claude, but I know it will give you pleasure to see it resting on her beautiful head" (46). Beatrice's discussion with Claude bears a remarkable resemblance to a historical occasion that Clayton records: "One evening, at the termination of the opera, the rival singers were called for, and a number of wreaths and bouquets were flung on the stage. One of the coronals fell at the feet of Malibran, who, considering it was meant for her, stooped and picked it up; when a stern voice from the pit cried out, 'Rendez-la: ce n'est pas pour vous!' 'I would not deprive Mdlle. Sontag of the coronal,' answered Malibran, somewhat scornfully; 'I would sooner bestow one on her' " (306). At the conclusion of Alcott's story, Beatrice rises to crown Theresa. She resumes her role as object of the audience's gaze. "Glittering with a strange magnificence," Beatrice is dressed in a velvet robe with "jewels sparkl[ing]" and "shin[ing] like stars in her dark hair" (50). When she crowns the head of Theresa, she crushes her to death "with the iron crown concealed among the roses on her blood-stained hair" (50).

Beatrice offers her floral crown out of despair. Having sacrificed the affections of her audience to Theresa for an unfaithful lover, Beatrice finds herself detached from both the public and private spheres. As Ackerman accurately observed, "Despite the self-conscious theatricality of the private sphere in late nineteenth-century America, Alcott's actresses ultimately fail to bridge the gap between domesticity and theatre. Their attempts lead to death, insanity or at least to the stigma of moral corruption" (182). Unable to claim an idyllic life in the domestic sphere, Beatrice returns to the public stage to enact her revenge. With the eyes of her adoring audience upon her for the last time, she delivers her final performance. She avenges her rival with an act worthy of the melodramas she embodied onstage—murder with a crown of roses.

Alcott does not conclude the story with the murder. Instead, she adds a postlude that makes Beatrice's fate explicit. The narrator explains: "Years passed away. In a lonely convent lived and died a sad, gray-haired man, worn and wasted with remorse, and in a quiet home for the insane dwelt a beautiful, pale woman who constantly wove garlands and, like a swan, died singing mournfully—and these were Claude and Beatrice" (50). Some critics assert that the final paragraph weakens the impact of the story's conclusion. While leaving Beatrice's mental stability in question, Alcott offers many clues that suggest her clear-headed sanity—even while committing an atrocious murder. Familiar with the language of opera, Alcott knew that the only voice of protest that female characters in most romantic operas were allowed was madness. The patriarchal power structure could explain and excuse the deviant actions of women by labeling it as madness. What if Alcott's postlude, rather than providing a simple fix to complex tensions in the narrative, offers a tongue-in-cheek gesture of defiance toward the patriarchal public sphere that controlled her own artistic voice? As Leonardi and Pope explain in *The Diva's Mouth: Body, Voice, and Prima Donna Politics*, "The diva's voice is a political force. It asserts equality and earns authority in the public, masculine world (one reason that, of course, masculine discourse must diminish it, other it, confine it, label it and the woman who possesses and wields it as 'unnatural' or 'demented')" (19). Beatrice speaks (through and, perhaps, for Alcott) with her final murderous act of madness.

When Theresa takes the stage just prior to her murder, she sings the role of Norma, Bellini's Druid high priestess. Known as one of opera's greatest tragedies, *Norma* tells of a lover scorned and revenge enacted. Alcott chooses to use this bel canto opera in her story for two reasons. First, she relies on her audience's recognition of the plot similarities between her story of the dueling divas and the rivalry between Norma and Adalgisa. In both tales, a love triangle leads to revenge and, ultimately, death. Second, as numerous opera critics have noted, in bel canto opera, the heroines often embody what Susan McClary calls a "musical representation of madwomen." She explains that when the "music is continually far in excess of the meanings of the lyrics" and the arias call for "coloratura delirium," all "qualities regarded as evidence of superior imagination—even of genius—in each period of music are, when enacted on stage, often projected onto madwomen" (McClary 92, 101). Unlike many of the typical romantic operas, *Norma* features a heroine who controls her own destiny rather than submitting to the will of a man. Although she dies at the end, Norma takes her own life. Similarly, one of Alcott's divas loses her life, but she is murdered by her rival—not her lover. Alcott reclaims the tradition of "feminine endings" by reversing our expectations.[5] The diva singing to her death dies by her rival's act of revenge, an act that appears to have been performed with forethought and malice, yet one that the spectators read as madness. Unknowingly, Claude provides the inspiration for her method when he says, "I shall indeed delight in seeing a wreath of your weaving on your rival's head [. . .] but put in no more roses, or you will crush instead of crown her, Beatrice, for this wreath, light as it is, will fall heavily from the height whence you will drop it on her head. It might be a pleasant death for one to die crushed with flowers in our hour of joy; but we cannot lose Theresa yet, so weave the garland lightly [. . .]" (47). After hearing his words, "she started and some dreadful thought seemed to flash into her mind. For her cheek grew paler still, a fierce, dark smile shot across her face, her eyes gleamed with sudden light, and her lips moved silently, as if she muttered spells above the flowers she wove" (47).

Alcott's allusion to *Norma* prepares the reader for her story's tragic ending. Although forbidden by her vow of chastity, Norma falls in love with Pollione, a Roman warrior and an enemy of her people. While Norma must keep her love for Pollione and the children she bore him a secret from her people, she still possesses an ardent affection for him. He, however, turns his attention to another young virgin of the temple of Irminsul, Adalgisa. When he admits that he has abandoned his love for Norma, a fellow soldier asks Pollione, "What 'count will ye render up to Norma?" Pollione replies: "Her vengeance, her anger, / Too dread for utt'rance, before my sight assemble; A vision: / Merely rememb'ring, / I tremble" (*Norma* 19). Recognizing that Norma's vengeance would be stirred greatly, he imagines:

> When an unearthly awful shade,
> Fashion'd, fashion'd itself from nothing,

Mists like a druid mantle laid
That vap'ry form were clothing;
Tempest his legion flames array'd,
Daylight shrank out all sickly,
Hideous 'mid darkness, thick
Sepulchred horrors move.
Vainly I sought the gentle one,
There at the altar kneeling,
Mocking my search, a stifled moan
On the sad air come stealing;
While in a deep mysterious tone
Re-echo'd thro' the temple,
"Norma, thus make example
Of traitors false to Love." (21–22)

Meanwhile, ignorant of Pollione's indiscretions, Norma secretly pleads for peace between Rome and the Druids while her people call for the slaughter of the Proconsul of Rome. In the well-known "Casta Diva" aria, Norma prays to the moon, the "Queen of Heaven" who is "clad in pureness, and disdaining / Grosser Earth's nocturnal veil" to "Let its essence, let its holier, sweeter essence / Quelling ev'ry unlawful license / [. . .] As above, above, so here, so here, prevail" (40–42). Even as her people cry for Pollione's blood, Norma longingly pleads, "Restore to mine affliction / One smile of love's protection, / My heart in thy (Pollione's) affection its only summer knows" (45). The chorus, however, sings of the ominous future for Norma and Pollione: "Well nurs'd in slumb'ring preparation, / War, blot out these cursed foes. / O vengeance" (48–49).

As a priestess, Adalgisa also breaks faith with her holy vow by entertaining Pollione's amorous overtures. When Adalgisa approaches Norma with a confession of her affair, she pleads to be released from her vow. Norma, remembering her own illicit love, shows mercy on Adalgisa and rescinds her obligations. When Norma discovers that Pollione is the young soldier that has captured Adalgisa's heart, however, her compassion turns to rage. Having risked everything to be with Pollione, she cannot bear his unfaithfulness.

With the discovery of Pollione's affair, the illusion of Norma's dreams has been shattered. Simultaneously endangering the lives of her people—the Druids—and the lives of her bastard children by inviting the wrath of Rome and of the gods, Norma realizes that she must take responsibility and rectify these wrongs. Almost driven to murder her own children—fearing the horrors they would face when the Druids learned they were fathered by a Roman—Norma entrusts their lives to her rival, Adalgisa. Recognizing that her god will demand a sacrifice, Norma prepares to offer herself on the pyre. Thinking that he will be the sacrifice, Pollione watches in amazement and admiration as Norma accepts responsibility for their love affair. In the final scene, Norma retains her dignity as she addresses Pollione with these final words:

> The deep affection
> Too ill requited,
> The burning passion
> So foully slighted,
> Yet seek to teach thee
> Falsehearted Roman
> The faith of woman
> Beyond the grave.
> Eternal ages
> Shall o'er us gather,
> Expire, and find us still link'd together:
> The heart that won me
> In love to languish,
> Death's lesser anguish
> With me must brave. (168–69)

Moved by her self-sacrifice and her steadfast love for him, Pollione cries,

> My soul so tardy
> Knew not to love thee,
> Sublimest angel,

> Too late I prove thee;
> Remorse hath prob'd me,
> Where truth was sleeping,
> Its purest weeping [. . .] (169),

and he joins Norma on the sacrificial pyre.

In "The Rival Prima Donnas," Alcott presents a heroine who refuses to be silenced. While the spectators interpret her actions as madness, Alcott undercuts that reading at every turn. When this diva asserts her voice in the final pages of the story, the public sphere hears it only as mad raging. Beatrice, however, will not be domesticated. Rewriting the nineteenth-century tradition that operas portray the "undoing" of women, Alcott offers a heroine who will not be silenced—even if the public sphere labels her insane and removes her from their gaze.

3

AN AWAKENING OF THE ARTIST

Opera in Chopin and Cather

In his essay "Religion and Art" (1880), Richard Wagner explained the vital role that art plays in articulating the essence of the human experience. "One might say that where Religion becomes artificial, it is reserved for Art to save the spirit of religion by recognizing the figurative value of the mythic symbols which the former would have us believe in their literal sense, and revealing their deep and hidden truth through an ideal presentation" (39). For Wagner, his art—his music—enabled him to speak about redemption and truth, freeing humanity from the encumbering servitude of the will. Writing and composing during the late nineteenth century, Wagner encountered an age of skepticism and change. "Many intellectuals of the nineteenth century had lost their faith in Christianity, together with their belief in the rational validity of any metaphysical knowledge. Thus bereft, they had to rely increasingly on the word of science. Science, particularly scientific determinism, however, could not provide complete and satisfactory answers to the questions of what is the nature of man, how ought human beings to treat one another, and how ought they to behave sexually" (Sessa 148).

In the late nineteenth century people's perceptions of themselves and their universe fundamentally changed. Even while advances were being made in science, psychology, and industry, some middle- and upper-class women experienced a "crisis of confinement and disutility" (Horowitz 7). They faced "restrictions on travel (no solo journeys), on attire (layers of restrictive undergarments), [and] on self-expression (no discussion of sexual needs)," which "contributed to an epidemic of 'neurasthenia'—by which term doctors diagnosed nervous prostration and other symptoms of irrelevance" (Horowitz 10). During this same period, two female American writers—Kate Chopin and Willa Cather—were struggling to embrace the vocation of literary artist that had been primarily reserved for men. Finding that creative genius has been "heavily gendered," Carolyn Korsmeyer explains that, "throughout its protean history, genius has been the proper possession of men." That "reverence for creative artistic imagination," she maintains, "burgeoned in the Romantic period" (156).

Struggling to find a voice, female writers searched for a source of artistic inspiration. In Wagner's music, American women discovered an outlet for their untapped creativity. According to Joseph Horowitz, "The cult of Wagner [. . .] powerfully infiltrated the women's movement—most American Wagnerites were female [. . .]" (2). Wagner offered "an avenue of intense spiritual experience, a surrogate for religion or cocaine, a song of redemption to set beside Emerson and Whitman" (Horowitz 8). Instead of imitating the standard models of popular opera, Wagner's art was innovative. Sparking controversy, his operas offered audiences passion and sensuality, yet they were also intellectually stimulating. Wagnerian operas illustrated that the art form could thrill mind, body, and spirit. According to Wagner, attending an opera should be a kind of religious experience. As the first operatic composer to "introduce the darkened theater and hidden orchestra" while "insisting on a silent audience during performances," Wagner promoted "the intimacy and solemnity of the event" (Harbison 150). This atmosphere allowed the action on stage to transcend a performance and serve as a "transformative experience that would, in the medieval sense, 'ravish the soul' " (Harbison 150). Therefore, it is not surprising that in Wagner's operas, Chopin and Cather discovered a language for articulating the awakening of the female artist.

Reenvisioning opera as *Gesamtkunstwerk*, Wagner integrated poetry, music, and drama into a unified, epic work of art. In *Opera and Drama* (1851), Wagner asserts that "*Music is a woman*," and "the nature of Woman is *love:* but this love is a *receiving* (*empfangende*), and in receival (*Empfängniss*) an unreservedly *surrendering*, love" (111). Using this metaphor, he explains the distinction between his operas and the more familiar Italian, French, and German forms. Italian opera, Wagner claims, is a "*wanton.*" The wanton is "an undeveloped, wasted woman: yet she at least fulfills the physical functions of the female sex, by which we can still—albeit with regret—detect the Woman in her" (112). Wagner identifies French opera with a "*coquette.*" He explains that "the coquette loves from thievish Egoism, and her vital force is icy coldness. In *her* the nature of Woman is perverted to its odious opposite; from her chilling smile, which only mirrors back our broken likeness, we turn mayhap, in desperation, to the Italian wanton" (112–13). While these characterizations are clearly critical, Wagner reserves his most blistering criticism for "the so-called German opera-music." To this type he levies the label of prude, the "type that fills us with the utmost horror" because "the prude fall[s] headlong into all the vices of her French and Italian sisters,—only, still further tainted by the arch-vice of hypocrisy, and alas without one glimmer of originality!" (114).

As his unfavorable portrayals indicate, Wagner found the existing opera forms woefully inadequate. He anticipates the question, "What kind of woman must true music be?" (115).

> A woman *who really loves,* who sets her virtue in her *pride,* however, in her *sacrifice;* that sacrifice whereby she surrenders, not *one portion* of her being, but *her whole being* in the amplest fullness of its faculty—when she *conceives.* But in joy and gladness to *bear* the thing conceived, this is *the deed* of Woman,—and to work deeds the woman only needs *to be entirely what she is,* but in no way *to will* something: for she can will but one thing—*to be a woman*! (114–15)

Following Wagner's metaphor, in order for conception to occur, the woman (music) needs a lover. In Wagner's operas, music's lover is the poet. As he explains, "If Poet and Musician, however, do not restrict each other, but rouse each other's powers into highest might, by Love; if in this Love they are all that ever they can be; if they *mutually go under* in the offering that each brings each,—the offering of his very highest potence,—then the Drama in its highest plentitude is born" (353). The offspring of music and poetry's coupling is Drama. Bringing together all of these elements—music, poetry, and drama—Wagner creates his "total artwork." Unlike many of his operatic predecessors, Wagner served as composer and librettist, orchestrating all the compositional elements of each work.

Wagner's *Gesamtkunstwerk* transformed the structure of opera, and it also underscored the vital link between art and religion. In an open letter to opera-star Lillian Nordica, published in the Lincoln, Nebraska, *Courier* on December 16, 1899, Willa Cather's description of the power of music (written at age twenty-six) echoes Wagner's characterization of his "total artwork": "Yet, forget it not, music first came to us many a century ago [. . .] as a religious chant and a love song. I believe that through all its evolutions it should always express those two cardinal needs of humanity, carrying the echo of those yearnings which first broke the silence of the world" (*World* 2: 645). According to Wagner, only the artist possesses a "clear eye" capable of "spy[ing] out shapes that reveal themselves to a yearning which longs for the only truth—*the human being*" (*Opera* 2: 375). Wagner believed that in the marriage of music, poetry, and drama, art would find its consummate expression. Not surprisingly, when Kate Chopin and Willa Cather wrote about the artist's awakening, they appropriated Wagnerian opera in fiction as a way of illustrating the connection between divinity and artistry. As her 1925 preface to Gertrude Hall's *Wagnerian Romances* suggests, Cather viewed Wagnerian opera as an exemplary form of literary and musical expression. "In the Wagnerian music-drama the literary part of the work is not trivial," she explains, "but is truly the mate of the music, done by the same hand" ("Preface" viii). Cather felt a special kinship with Wagner as a fellow literary artist. She believed that art and religion offered to humanity the only real glimpses of immortal beauty. The deity, for Cather, is this "Painter, this Poet, this Musician, this gigantic Artist of all art that is, this God whose spirit moved upon chaos leaving beauty incarnate in its shadow [. . .]" (*Kingdom* 178). In Wagner's music, Cather and Chopin discovered a language for articulating the artist's identity and her struggles.

Cather and Chopin would transform the American literary landscape by replacing the traditional male *Bildungsroman* with narratives about a female artist's growth. Chopin's *The Awakening* and Cather's

The Song of the Lark may be characterized as *Künstlerromans,* "tale[s] of a young woman who struggles to realize herself—and her artistic ability." In addition, these novels "reveal something of [each] author's own struggle, and, what is more important, something of the struggle of all women artists" (Huf 69). Susan Rosowski offers a helpful definition of the "novel of awakening."

> The subject and the action of the novel of awakening characteristically consist of a protagonist who attempts to find value in a world defined by love and marriage. The direction of the awakening follows what is becoming a pattern in literature by and about women: movement is inward, toward greater self knowledge that leads in turn to a revelation of the disparity between that self knowledge and the nature of the world. The protagonist's growth results typically not with "an art of living," as for her male counterpart, but instead with a realization that for a woman such an art of living is difficult or impossible: it is an awakening to limitations. (313)

Despite the constraints that nineteenth-century culture imposed on aspiring female artists, Chopin managed to carve a space out of her domestic duties for developing her own literary talent. She did not have to imagine the limitations facing the female artists; she lived them: marriage, family, economic necessity. Against all odds, however, Chopin recognized "what feminists only recently have come to articulate fully: the intimate connection between body and the unconscious activity that produces art" (Weatherford 103). "Writing in a period of transition in terms of the 'woman question' " (Foster 155), Chopin published *The Awakening* in 1899. Although for many years Chopin was dismissed as a local colorist, purely a regional writer, that view has changed in the last four decades. One aspect of the work that remains largely unexplored, however, is the significance of Wagner's *Tristan and Isolde* within the novel.

Like several of her fellow nineteenth-century writers, Chopin displayed an affinity for music, particularly opera. Chopin possessed a sophisticated knowledge of music. Biographers Emily Toth and Per Seyersted observe that "Kate Chopin was a lover of music all her life.

When she was a child at the Sacred Heart Academy, her mother paid for her to take extra piano lessons. As an adolescent, Kate O'Flaherty also attended the St. Louis Academy of the Visitation for extra musical training. She could read music, and could also repeat, by ear, opera music she had heard" (195). Not coincidentally, her first publication was a piece of music, the "Lilia. Polka for the Piano," published by H. H. Rollman and Sons, St. Louis, in 1888 (195). In her commonplace book, begun in 1867 as an assignment for Mary O'Meara, one of the nuns at Sacred Heart, Chopin records numerous occasions when she attended musical performances, including opera and parlor concerts. She also remembers an incident when she entertained a rather disagreeable guest by playing the piano as "the most pleasing way both to himself and me of fulling [*sic*] my mission of entertainer. Wishing to suit his taste what ever it might be—I played pieces of every variety: Operas—Sonatas—Meditations—Galops—Nocturnes—Waltzes & Jigs—after accompanying which—I turned to him" (Toth and Seyersted 17).

In her honeymoon diary, "Three Months Abroad," Chopin recalls attending the opera with her husband, Oscar, on July 16, 1870. She writes: "Walked about town rather listlessly to day [*sic*]. In the morning went to the boiling springs tasted the water and thought it shocking. Oscar of course found it delicious. Dined at 6. and afterwards went to the Opera to hear the in comparable [*sic*] Wm. Tell. How I could & how I would have enjoyed it, had I felt better; but have been feeling badly all day. To morrow [*sic*] en route for Frankfurt" (Toth and Seyersted 108–9). Carol Corum notes that the Chopins, "while on their honeymoon in 1870, were hearing the Theodore Thomas Orchestra in its fifth season and were being a part of not only the orchestra's early popularity but also Wagner's early popularity" (37). Seyersted suggests that Chopin's love of Wagner deepened in New Orleans, where she lived from 1870 to 1879. "While Kate Chopin took advantage of the entertainment afforded by the New Orleans panorama of human nature, she no doubt also made every use of what the city's Academy of Music, two opera houses, and several theaters had to offer. Edwin Booth, Sarah Bernhardt, and other great artists performed here, and the French Opera House was the first in America to stage such works as *Lohengrin* and *Tannhäuser*" (42). Just as New

Orleans residence exposed Chopin to various opera productions, so did her return to St. Louis. After her husband's death in 1882, Chopin came back to St. Louis in mid-1884, living there until 1904. Seyersted notes that "St. Louis had two opera companies and a Philharmonic Society" (24). In addition, Chopin could have attended the performances delivered in St. Louis by the Metropolitan Opera's touring company during its 1885–86 German opera season. Those tours featured five Wagner operas—*Rienzi, Tannhäuser, Lohengrin, Die Walküre,* and *Die Meistersinger.* In 1891, Chopin delivered a paper on "Typical Forms of German Music" at a Wednesday Club meeting in St. Louis, but the text is now lost. In 1899, *The Atlantic* published Chopin's "The Typical German Composers" (Toth, "Kate Chopin's Music" 28).

Chopin's knowledge of contemporary opera music is reflected by her having the Farival twins in *The Awakening* play a duet from *Zampa,* a romantic opera by Louis Hérold. *Zampa* was one of the "four most successful operas-comique of the period" (Corum 37–38). The most significant use of opera in *The Awakening,* however, is not as explicit. Wagner's influence on the text pervades the entire narrative even though his opera remains unnamed. When Mademoiselle Reisz "glided from the Chopin into the quivering love-notes of Isolde's song, and back again to the Impromptu with its soulful and poignant longing," she introduces a work from Wagner's *Tristan and Isolde* (1865). But, the narrative relationship of "deferral and fulfillment" of desire (Kramer, *Music* 154) exists long before Chopin alludes directly to "The Transfiguration" from *Tristan and Isolde.* Chopin's fiction imitates what Wagner's music achieves: "deferral acts as a means by which the story of desire is prolonged" (154). Unlike the opera, however, the ultimate goal for Chopin's heroine is not a consummation of desire for a lover; rather, she seeks a transcendent freedom and independence from the traditional roles she embodies.

Chronicling Edna Pontellier's interior journey of consciousness, *The Awakening* traces the twenty-eight-year-old wife and mother's realization of her own artistry, freedom, and passion. Unlike the literary models of her male counterparts, Edna's is "an awakening to limitations" (Rosowski 313). A native Kentuckian, Edna marries Léonce Pontellier, a New Orleans French Creole brokerage businessman, and assumes the role of an aristocratic lady. As such, she manages the household servants, looks after the welfare of her two sons, Raoul and Etienne, and observes reception day on Tuesday afternoon. "On Tuesday afternoons," the narrator explains, "there was a constant stream of callers—women who came in carriages or in the street cars, or walked when the air was soft and distance permitted" (Chopin 50). Edna has followed this "programme" (50) for six years—ever since her marriage. The novel portrays Edna, however, as ill at ease in all of these roles. She is "not a mother-woman" (10), and the responsibility for her children is one "she had blindly assumed and for which Fate had not fitted her" (20). While "it would have been a difficult matter for Mr. Pontellier to define to his own satisfaction or any one else's wherein his wife failed in her duty toward their children," nevertheless "it was something which he felt rather than perceived" (9). Edna's inefficiencies as a household manager are illustrated by Léonce's rebuke about the cook's performance: "cooks are only human. They need looking after, like any other class of persons that you employ. Suppose I didn't look after the clerks in my office, just let them run things their own way; they'd soon make a nice mess of me and my business" (52).

As the novel soon reveals, Edna fails in these traditional roles because she longs for independence, passion, and self-expression. Stifled by the too tightly defined life she leads, she begins exploring a life beyond the confines of her marriage. Her awakening to self begins with a friendship she establishes with Robert Lebrun, a twenty-six-year-old bachelor, during the family's vacation on the Grand Isle. Robert has a reputation as being "the devoted attendant of some fair dame or damsel" (12) each summer, and the other vacationers rarely take his attentions to the women too seriously. At his urging, Edna accepts the "imperative entreaty" of the Gulf's waters. Under the spell of the water's murmurs and with the companionship of Robert, Edna begins "to realize her position in the universe as a human being, and to recognize her relations as an individual to the world within and about her" (15). Described by Chopin as "the beginning of things, of a world especially," Edna's awakening to self is "necessarily vague, tangled, chaotic, and exceedingly disturbing" (15)—much like the water of the sea. In a Wagnerian description, Chopin's narrator suggests that "the voice of the sea is seductive; never ceasing, whispering, clamoring, murmuring, inviting the soul to wander for a spell in abysses of solitude; to lose itself in mazes of inward contemplation. The voice of the sea speaks to the soul. The touch of the sea is sensuous, enfolding the body in its soft, close embrace" (15).

In the description of the sensuous fluidity of the sea, Chopin characterizes desire in Freudian terms. Sigmund Freud's *Three Contributions to the Theory of Sex* (1910) provided a psychobiological model of desire that "differs from its classical predecessor in only one essential respect, but that one is explosive. Instead of understanding desire as a recurrent disposition of the body," Freud proposed that it is "a persistent force within the personal subject." Based on this understanding, "desire becomes a basic component of subjectivity itself, one of the cluster of basic forces that establishes subjectivity as the chief institution of personhood" (Kramer, *Music* 137). Libido, Freud suggested, "is preeminently *fluid*" (Kramer, *Music* 141). Replacing the classical model of desire—fire—the metaphor of fluidity influenced several nineteenth-century artists. In *Tristan and Isolde,* Wagner offers "a musical realization of this idea [desire as endless ebbing and flowing]" (Kramer, *Music* 147). Nietzsche described the effect of Wagner's opera in this way:

> One walks into the sea, gradually loses one's secure footing, and finally surrenders oneself to the elements without reservation: one must *swim.* In older music, what one had to do [. . .] was something quite different, namely, to *dance.* The measure required for this, the maintenance of certainly equally balanced units of time and force, demanded continual wariness of the listener's soul—and on the counterplay of this cooler breeze that came from *wariness* and the warm breath of enthusiasm rested the magic of all *good* music. Richard Wagner wanted a different kind of movement; he overthrew the physiological presupposition of previous music. Swimming, floating—no longer walking and dancing. (qtd. in Horowitz 110–11)

Edna's epiphanies always occur in the waves: swimming in the

Gulf's waves with Lebrun and listening to the waves of sound as Mademoiselle Reisz plays the piano. When Edna learns to swim, she ventures out alone in the water and "turn[s] her face seaward to gather in an impression of space and solitude, which the vast expanse of water, meeting and melting with the moonlit sky, convey[s] to her excited fancy." In the embrace of the ocean, Edna "reach[es] out for the unlimited in which to lose herself" (29). Just as the embrace of the ocean stirs Edna's passions, so, too, do the chords offered by Mademoiselle Reisz, a musical artist. Before hearing her play the piano, "musical strains had a way of evoking pictures in [Edna's] mind" (26). Hearing Reisz's notes, however, "the very passions themselves were aroused within her soul, swaying it, lashing it, as the waves daily beat upon her splendid body. She trembled, she was choking, and the tears blinded her" (27). The metaphoric fluidity of water provides Chopin with the language to describe Edna's awakening to self.

In an effort to discover the essential self, Edna explores the possibility of turning her "dabbling" (13) with the paintbrushes into a vocation. Possessing a "natural aptitude," Edna handles her brushes "with a certain ease and freedom" (13). Previously, however, Edna painted for pleasure during her leisure hours. Feeling "as if [she] wanted to be doing something" (55), Edna "gathered together a few of the sketches—those which she considered the least discreditable" (54), hoping they merited further study with a professional artist, Laidpore. Her efforts eventually are rewarded with success. As Edna reports, "I am beginning to sell my sketches. Laidpore is more and more pleased with my work; he says it grows in force and individuality. I cannot judge that for myself, but I felt that I have gained in ease and confidence. [. . .] I know I shall like it, like the feeling of freedom and independence" (79). While Edna's decision to pursue a self-supporting vocation is shocking enough for her husband and friends, choosing painting is even more scandalous. Germaine Greer observes in *The Obstacle Race: The Fortunes of Women Painters and Their Work* that, "as the chief source of inspiration to male painters, the beauty of women had condemned them to the passive role." Despite their best efforts, most art patrons continued to believe that "women artists were not as men struggling to find the means of giving aesthetic expression to visions of an object of universal desire"; instead, the female artists were themselves "the objects of aesthetic desire. The young woman who gave evidence of talent was not an artist, but a muse" (Greer 72). In addition, "one of the characteristics which women were expected to bring to their art was purity" (Greer 319). Because "female sensuality was repugnant to accepted taste," it was also "inaccessible to most female artists" (Greer 320). Edna, however, does not allow these limitations to deter her. Kindled by a passion that Robert Lebrun's attentions have sparked, Edna forges ahead with her art.

Pursuing her painting, however, does not entirely fulfill Edna's desires. Harboring an unrequited passion for Lebrun, she hungers for any word of him. Her search takes her to Mademoiselle Reisz's abode. In response to Reisz's inquiries, Edna exclaims, "I am becoming an artist. Think of it!" (63). Reisz replies that "You have pretensions, Madame. [. . .] To be an artist includes much; one must possess many gifts—absolute gifts—which have not been acquired by one's own effort. And, moreover to succeed, the artist must possess the courageous soul. [. . .] Courageous, *ma foi*! The brave soul. The soul that dares and defies" (63). As Edna learns, this courage steels the artist for a life of solitude. Early in the novel, the narrator portrays Reisz as a loner, a solitary figure, but the description of the pianist is unflattering: "She was a disagreeable little woman, no longer young, who had quarreled with almost every one, owing to a temper which was self-assertive and a disposition to trample upon the rights of others. [. . .] She was a homely woman, with a small weazened face and body and eyes that glowed. She had absolutely no taste in dress, and wore a batch of rusty black lace with a bunch of artificial violets pinned to the side of her hair" (26). The antithesis of sensuality in her appearance, Mademoiselle Reisz stirs Edna's passion when she plays the piano. Mademoiselle Reisz, "by her divine art," speaks to "Edna's spirit and set[s] it free" (78), encouraging Edna to "resolve never again to belong to another than herself" (80). Listening to Chopin's "Impromptu" and Wagner's "Transfiguration," Edna is moved to tears. The music awakens the deep longing that Edna first felt on the shores of Grand Isle: "The shadows deepened in the little room. The music grew strange and fantastic—turbulent, insistent, plaintive and soft with entreaty" (64).

Although Chopin refers to the piece as "Isolde's Song," the selection Mademoiselle Reisz plays is actually "The Transfiguration" from Richard Wagner's *Tristan and Isolde.* As the recurrent motif of water imagery, the movement of longing and yearning, and Edna's final enfolding into the sea indicate, the reverberations of *Tristan and Isolde* are evident throughout the novel, not just in the scene alluding to it. In *Tristan and Isolde,* Wagner effectively illustrates the nature of desire—an endless ebbing and flowing. Lawrence Kramer observes, "The musical realization of this idea [desire as endless ebbing and flowing] depends on a cluster of distinctive effects: melodic motion by semitones, ambiguous or indefinite harmonies, a texture dense with appoggiaturas, many of which 'resolve' to unstable referential sonorities" (*Music* 147). Simultaneously, the opera holds in tension two opposing forces—the fulfillment of desire and the deferral of desire. Wagner achieves this musically by offering "a passage that reaches a climactic melodic cadence at the same time as it defaults on a full harmonic cadence" (148). The effect on opera's audience is a prolonged sense of yearning for resolution—both harmonic and narrative. Just as Tristan and Isolde wait to be joined with one another, the audience waits for a resolution of harmony, melody, and text. Kramer explains how Wagner achieves this goal.

> It is at Tristan's death that Wagner begins the restructuring of the Lust-trope that will come to fruition in the Transfiguration. Isolde, arrived from Cornwall at last, holds the dying Tristan in her arms while the Prelude is recapitulated from the Desire motive to the F-major deceptive cadence and a little beyond. At first the music is very loud and agitated; Tristan, after all, is dying at the very moment of reunion. Yet the clamor and agitation steadily subside, as does the tempo, yielding at last to a tranquility that irradiates the cadence. In another instance of expansion into "measureless space," Wagner gives the cadence an unprecedented breadth, sustaining its B [flat] appoggiatura many times longer than he does in the Prelude. The swell of desire is correspondingly fuller, its melodic resolution more gratifying, its accentuation of the pitch b2 the more telling.

> The lovers may be cheated of each other after the agonies of anticipation, yet their separation draws to a focus in the primary form of the *Lust*-trope, music that embodies the life, not the death, of libidinal desire. (*Music* 159)

In his program notes, Wagner describes the power of *Tristan and Isolde.*

> Here in music's own most unrestricted element, the musician who chose this for the introduction to his drama of love could have but one care: how to impose restraint on himself, since exhaustion of the subject is impossible. So just once, in one long-articulated impulse, he let that insatiable longing swell up from the timidest avowal of the most delicate attraction, through anxious sighs, hopes and fears, laments and wishes, raptures and torments, to the mightiest onset and to the most powerful effort to find the breach that will reveal to the infinitely craving heart the path into the sea of love's endless rapture. In vain! Its power spent, the heart sinks back to languish in longing, in longing without attainment, since each attainment brings in its wake only renewed desire, until in final exhaustion the breaking glance catches a glimmer of the attainment of highest rapture: it is the rapture of dying, of ceasing to be, of the final redemption into that wondrous realm from which we stray the furthest when we strive to enter it by force. Shall we call it Death? Or is it the miraculous world of Night, from which, as the story tells, an ivy and a vine sprang of old in inseparable embrace over the grave of Tristan and Isolde? (*Prelude* 48)

By labeling Isolde's final song as "The Transfiguration," Wagner clearly rebukes any critics who might view her death as an end to the love and passion she has shared with Tristan. Instead, the negation of life offers an opportunity for transcendence to a spiritual and sensual union. Traditionally, Isolde's concluding monologue has been inaccurately identified as the *Liebestod.*[1] Wagner, however, consistently referred to this piece as "The Transfiguration," and in the program notes he describes the work: "Yet what Fate divided in life now springs into transfigured life in death: the gates of union are thrown open. Over Tristan's body the dying Isolde receives the blessed fulfillment of ardent longing, eternal union in measureless space, without barriers, without fetters, inseparable!" (48). In Isolde's, and the opera's, concluding words it is evident that in her "drowning" she finally achieves the fulfillment that eluded her in life.

> Mildly, gently,
> See him smiling,
> See his eyes
> Softly open.
> Ah behold him!
> See you not?
> Ever brighter,
> Brightly shining,
> Borne in starlight
> High above?
> See you not?
> How his heart
> So proudly swells,
> Full and bold
> It throbs in his breast?
> Gentle breathing
> Stirs his lips,
> Ah, how calmly
> Soft his breath:—
> See him, friends!
> Feel and see you not?
> Can it be that I alone
> Hear this wondrous, glorious tone,
> Softly stealing,
> All revealing,
> Mildly glowing,
> From him flowing,
> Thro' me pouring,

Rising, soaring,
Boldly singing,
Round me ringing?
Brighter growing,
O'er me flowing,
Are they waves
Of tender radiance?
Are they clouds
Of wonderful fragrance?
They are rising
High around me,
Shall I breathe them,
Shall I hear them?
Shall I taste them?
Dive beneath them?
Drown in tide
Of melting sweetness?
In the rapturous swell,
In the turbulent spell,
In the welcoming wave,
Holding all.
I'm sinking,
I'm drowning,
Unaware,
Highest love! (92)

Despite the clear influence of *Tristan and Isolde* upon *The Awakening*, many critics refrain from asserting that the concluding scene of Chopin's novel reenacts "The Transfiguration." Edna's final journey into the water's embrace has been interpreted in a variety of ways. One difference from Wagner's scene is clear; Edna does not pursue a union with a lover. In the concluding scene, having abandoned the various lovers in her life—her husband, Léonce; her lover, Alcée Arobin; and her true love, Robert Lebrun—Edna enters the waters alone. When Robert returns to New Orleans from Mexico, Edna hopes to pursue a life with him. "I love you, and only you; no one but you. It was you who awoke me last summer out of a life-long, stupid dream. Oh! You have made me so unhappy with your indifference. Oh! I have suffered, suffered! Now you are here we shall love each other, my Robert. We shall be everything to each other. Nothing else in the world is of any consequence" (107). Yet, despite her highest hopes and his ardent longing for her, he refuses to become involved in a relationship, bidding her "Good by—because I love you" (111). Although Edna realizes that she possesses something of consequence—her sons, Raoul and Etienne, she vows to her friend Adéle Ratignolle that "she would never sacrifice herself for her children" (113). With "despondency," Edna walks down to the shore of the Gulf, recognizing that "there was no one thing in the world that she desired. There was no human being whom she wanted near her except Robert; and she even realized that the day would come when he, too, and the thought of him would melt out of her existence, leaving her alone" (113). Edna's awakening leaves her in a world of solitude. As she gains freedom and pursues the life of the artist, she discovers that her ties to family and friends are strained. Chopin subtitled the novel "A Solitary Soul," suggesting that Edna's ultimate self-realization is characterized not only by independence but also by isolation. Edna attempts to escape solitude by exploring her sexuality with Arobin, but she soon discovers that these sexual encounters—devoid of real love or affection—fail to dispel the emptiness she feels. Bound by the ties of husband and children, Edna cannot fully experience the solitary life of the artist as Mademoiselle Reisz does, so she seeks solitude in the only avenue she has left: death.

How should readers interpret Edna's death? Chopin provides a hint when she chooses "Isolde's Song" as the piece that Mademoiselle Reisz plays for Edna. By invoking Wagner's *Tristan and Isolde,* Chopin forces the reader to consider the implications of suicide in a complicated way. Neither Wagner nor Chopin use the term *death* to describe what happens to their heroines. In Wagner's opera, the stage directions simply state that "Isolde sighs in ecstasy, held in Brangäne's arms, and sinks upon Tristan's body. Profound emotion and grief of the bystanders. Mark calls down a blessing on the dead" (92). In Chopin's novel, "the shore was far behind [Edna], and her strength was gone. [. . .] She looked back into the distance, the old terror flamed up for an instant, then sank again" (114).

The details that conclude the novel are images from her memory:

"Edna heard her father's voice and her sister Margaret's. She heard the barking of an old dog that was chained to the sycamore tree. The spurs of the cavalry officer clanged as he walked across the porch. There was the hum of bees, and the musky odor of pinks filled the air" (114). Although some critics focus on the initial "despondency" that Edna experiences prior to this scene, Chopin does not conclude the novel with those emotions. Instead, the final words and images echo Edna's first impressions of the sea. Repeating those earlier phrases, the narrator reports, "The water of the Gulf stretched out before [Edna], gleaming with the million lights of the sun. The voice of the sea is seductive, never ceasing, whispering, clamoring, murmuring, inviting the soul to wander in abysses of solitude" (113). The call to solitude is an invitation, and although Edna cannot accept the solitary condition in life, she finds the sea's summons irresistible. "Leaving her clothing in the bath-house," Edna stands beside the sea, "absolutely alone" (113). Embracing this solitude for the first time, Edna "cast the unpleasant, pricking garments from her, and for the first time in her life she stood naked in the open air, at the mercy of the sun, the breeze that beat upon her, and the waves that invited her" (113). She thinks, "How strange and awful it seemed to stand naked under the sky! how delicious! She felt like some new-born creature, opening its eyes in a familiar world that it had never known" (113). The description of Edna's acceptance of the sea's invitation is not filled with desperation or despondency. Instead, the experience fills Edna with wonder, awe, and a sense of renewed possibilities. Her trip into the water offers her a chance to be reborn as the solitary creature of art that she longs to be. Whereas the embraces of human flesh have failed to fulfill her, she discovers that "the touch of the sea is sensuous, enfolding the body in its soft, close embrace" (113). The language at the final moment is similar to Isolde's. Flowing from the dying Tristan's body, Isolde discovers "waves of tender radiance," and she chooses to

> drown in [the] tide
> Of melting sweetness?
> In the rapturous swell,
> In the turbulent spell,

> In the welcoming wave,
> Holding all." (Wagner, *Tristan* 92)

Like Edna, Isolde willingly offers herself to the tides, simultaneously finding herself "drowning" yet experiencing "highest love!" (92).

In *Diving Deep and Surfacing: Women Writers on Spiritual Quest*, Carol Christ acknowledges that Edna's death is a "spiritual triumph," but she also insists that it is a "social defeat in that by choosing death she admits that she cannot find a way to translate her spiritual awareness of her freedom and infinite possibilities into life and relationships with others" (39). The interpretative key that Christ lacks is the Wagner opera. If Christ were to read *The Awakening* through a Wagnerian lens, she would recognize that Edna's spiritual awakening is clearly not a defeat but a triumph of the solitary soul. Critic Kelley Griffith does consider the influence of Wagner on the novel, but she comes to a very different conclusion. "Edna's suicide is a perversion even of Isolde's song of love, because Edna rejects all human connection," Griffith claims. "Her suicide is a self-centered choice that seems almost an act of aggression against those who care for her, most of all her children. Instead of a transfiguration," she asserts, "her Liebestod is a disfiguration, a denial of meaning. As she [Edna] walks into the sea her 'song' is no longer of love but has become an incoherent stream of images and memories, like the parrot's discordant mutterings at the beginning of the novel" (153). Griffith's interpretation is marred, however, by her identifying "Isolde's Song" as "Liebestod," the love-death. When the piece is correctly identified as "The Transfiguration," Wagner's intentions become clear.

Isolde's final act is more than a sacrificial effort to join with her lover; it is a spiritual transcendence. As numerous Wagner scholars have noted, Schopenhauer's *Die Welt als Wille und Vorstellung* (1819) influenced the composer's ideology. Anne Sessa describes the essence of Schopenhauer's study: "For Schopenhauer, the world is the blind, tragic, striving of the will. If the world is will, then it is full of pain and suffering, for it is not possible to satisfy the demands of desire. Wisdom in man consists of transcending the absurd appetites of will and finding rest in contemplation. Often man's wisdom is only the rationalization of what the will has done; however, sometimes the intellect disobeys the will. It may therefore be possible to develop the power of the intellect or consciousness so that it can rise above the strivings of the will" (65–66). While Schopenhauer suggests transcending the flesh's desire as the path to contemplation, Wagner offers a revision of this mode in *Tristan*. Sherill Harbison notes that Wagner "proposed obsessive sexual love as a kind of redemption from desire, revamping the archetypal courtly love myth to embrace and flout the idea of renunciation in the same breath. Indeed, it was precisely this slippery mix of sensuality and spirituality that most aroused Wagner's audiences: the libretto spoke of salvation, but the music spoke quite a different language" (151).

When Chopin and Cather heard *Tristan and Isolde,* they discovered an outlet for the expression of their long pent-up passions and desires. In *Wagner Nights: An American History,* Joseph Horowitz describes the power of an actual performance of *Tristan and Isolde.*

> At the Met, Isolde's death-song, thrusting toward regions of oceanic wholeness, of womb-like security, of prepubescent play, was consummated by the hypnotic and statuesque Lilli Lehmann. The bad effects of husband and bedroom were silenced by a musical-dramatic orgasm as explicit and complete as any mortal intercourse. And Isolde's second-act duet with Tristan—their clandestine Love-Night, shutting out the world, beckoning dissolution—was a secret pact, a shared conspiracy with Wagner, with Seidl [the conductor], with the dissolving Seidlites. For the moment, the parlor spinet, the neurasthenia of the bedroom, were banished and forgotten. The Wagner pilgrims were addicted, body and soul. (216)

Chopin must have found Wagner's revision of Schopenhauer intoxicating. Without denying the struggles of the will, Wagner discovered a way to infuse sensuality with sexuality. Chopin's heroine learns that the negation of life in death provides the mode not only of a transformation of self but also of a transfiguration of the soul. In the final scene, Edna embraces the solitude that her art demanded.

Like Chopin, Willa Cather discovered that the female artist's life is a solitary one. Although Cather enjoyed the companionship of various female friends, she never married. In an interview Cather conducted with Olive Fremstad, a Wagnerian soprano, the diva articulated a philosophy that the two obviously shared: "We are born alone, we make our way alone, we die alone" ("Three American Singers" 42). Cather explains in the article that Fremstad "believes that the artist's quest is pursued alone, and that the highest rewards are, for the most part, enjoyed alone. She is not confident that much of the singer's best work ever crosses the footlights to the people who sit beyond" (42). Fremstad identifies herself as an aesthete, pursuing art for its own sake. Cather's companion Edith Lewis remembered, "It was not only as a great singer and actress that one admired Fremstad: she was above all a great artist, a great visionary in art. One felt always that her vision was greater than any human power could encompass or satisfy" (90). When Cather looked for a way to illustrate an artist's awakening, she chose an opera singer.

Although a great admirer of musical and theatrical arts, Cather elevated opera and the opera singer above other performatory art forms and other artists. "An opera singer must have more dramatic power than an actress. Singing is idealized speech, and, in order to preserve the proportion and harmony between words and actions, the acting which accompanies it must be ideal. A singer is on stage less than an actress, and she must do more when she is there. She must do in one gesture what the actress of spoken words does in many. . ." (*Kingdom* 216–17). Cather's comments about the challenges and privileges a diva experiences echo her own sentiments about writing in "The Novel Démeublé." The artist—writer or opera singer—must be capable of communicating a wide range of expressions and emotions to the audience. Each must work within a set of constraints. As Cather explained, she must "present [the] scene by suggestion rather than by enumeration" (*Not Under Forty* 48). While the fiction writer and the opera diva face similar artistic challenges, they also share in one unique privilege, the ability to enter into the identity of another human being. Elizabeth Shepley Sergeant relates Cather's remarks about this capacity: "Novelists, opera singers, even doctors, [. . .] have in common the unique and marvelous experience of entering into the very skin of another human being. What can compare with it?" (48). The fiction writer and the musical performer must recreate human experience in order to move their audiences to recognition.

Embracing art, the diva offers herself as a vessel for the transmission of stirring emotion and sublime beauty. Cather underscores the power of the diva not only in her fiction but also in her prose articles and essays about art. The opera singer's power rests in her ability to stir the emotions. Describing her first experiences in the Red Cloud Opera House, Cather explains that "living people were making us feel things, and it is through the feelings, not at all through the eye, that one's imagination is fired" ("Incomparable" 376). The opera singer's voice served as an imaginative source of creativity for Cather, and it became her "recurrent metonymy for the woman artist" (O'Brien 166). The diva, temporarily living in the skin of another human being, gives life and voice to anger, fear, love, and longing. She shows the possibility of art's creating and recreating life rather than merely mirroring it. For Cather, the most authentic expressions of art unfold when "[. . .] a story of human experience (is) given to us alive, given to us, not only by voice and attitude, but by all those unnamed ways in which an animal of any species makes known its terror or misery to other animals of its kind" ("Incomparable" 376). Sharon O'Brien explains that "opera singers did not simply represent female art, as did the woman author's name on the title page. They incarnated it. An abstraction—female creativity—became tangible and credible in their presence" (O'Brien 167).

In March 1906 Cather moved to New York to accept a position as associate editor of *McClure's* magazine. Edith Lewis, Cather's companion, recalled that they "went constantly to the opera at this time." As Lewis notes, Cather's career in New York coincided with "one of the great periods of opera in New York." Lewis records many of the names of the leading opera stars of the time:

> Nordica and the de Reszkes, Melba and Calvé were still singing during our first years in New York. From 1905 on our old programmes continually list such names as Sembrich, Farrar,

> Chaliapin, Plançon, Destinn, Renaud, Mary Garden, Caruso, Amato, Homer, and Tetrazzini. Toscanini, not then half so famous, but at the height of his powers, was conducting two or three times a week at the Metropolitan. But the most thrilling, to us, of all the new stars that came up over the horizon was Olive Fremstad. We heard her nearly every time she sang. (90)

During the time that she lived with Lewis in a New York apartment at 5 Bank Street (1912–1927), Cather published *The Song of the Lark* (1915), a novel that features an opera singer as the central character and the embodiment of the artist. Lewis notes that "it was her [Cather's] intense preoccupation with opera at that time, and her great admiration for Mme. Fremstad, and interest in her complex personality, that gave the core of its inspiration to *The Song of the Lark*" (92). Lewis, like Cather, insists that "*Thea* is not a portrait of Fremstad—that many other elements enter into the character, especially much of Willa Cather's own childhood and youth; but *Thea* as a singer, and particularly in the latter part of the book, was directly suggested by Fremstad" (92–93). Apparently, Fremstad "recognized herself in *Thea* when she read the story," supposedly telling Cather that "she could not tell where *Thea* left off and she began" (93).

In the preface to *The Song of the Lark*, Cather explains that she "wanted to call the story 'Artist's Youth,' " but her publisher discouraged her. With that title, Cather hoped to "suggest a young girl's awakening to something beautiful" (v). Despite the altered title, within the novel's many details of Thea Kronborg's life—from her childhood to her pinnacle as a great opera singer—the quest for art emerges as the primary theme. Cather's epic novel recounts a creation story: the creation of an artist. "Every artist makes himself born," Harsanyi, Thea's piano teacher in Chicago, recounts. "It is very much harder than the other time, and, longer" (*Song* 221). Unlike her first birth, the artist's rebirth requires her own labor and sacrifice to bring forth her art and develop the artistic identity. In order for the artist to be reborn, all the priorities of life must be recentered. "The marriage between life and art is brought about through the sublimation of life into art," explains Richard Giannone (90).[2] The distinction between life and art blurs.

Not surprisingly, Cather's heroine is a Wagnerian soprano, further emphasizing the transforming power of art.

Cather knew about the struggle to find an artistic voice, and she chose the "diva's singing voice to explore the possibility of a woman's 'having a voice'—having power in the sense of both control and creation—outside the domestic sphere" (Leonardi 66). Inextricably tied to her identity as an artist, the diva's authority onstage influences not only the interpretation of the musical composition but also the emotional effect on the audience. As Susan Leonardi effectively argues in "To Have a Voice: The Politics of the Diva," the diva's voice functions on many levels. The voice, as a musical instrument, allows its mistress "participation, control, power, [and] creation" (69). Working as a creative artist, the diva relies upon the skills of improvisation and embellishment to relate her own unique interpretation of the music to her audience. Her artistic vision then becomes reenvisioned in the minds of her listeners. The voice of the opera singer possesses the "power to change the lives of those who hear her, but especially to change the lives of other women, to give them a voice in all senses" (Leonardi 71). As Cather explains, the diva's artistic interpretation of the music "speaks directly to them [the audience] *viva voce* and it must rouse their strongest emotions, stir their holiest memories. The artist whom the people love must feel, interpret, create" (*Kingdom* 217).

Thea Kronborg's awakening, from the Moonstone child into the Metropolitan Opera star, requires the development of an artistic soul and a singular passion. Although she is already "uncommon in a common, common world" (*Song* 268), Thea must claim her identity as an artist. Harsanyi, Thea's piano teacher in Chicago, asks her when she first realized that she wanted to be an artist. She replies, "I don't know. There was always—something" (264). With further prompting, she admits that she always knew she would sing. Just as her first piano teacher Wunsch remarked, "Some things cannot be taught. If you not know in the beginning, you not know in the end. For a singer there must be something in the inside from the beginning" (98). Everyone who encounters Thea recognizes the spark of greatness and artistry within her. She impresses her lover, Fred Ottenburg, "as equipped to be an artist, and to be nothing else; already directed, concentrated, formed as to mental habit" (421). Although Cather suggests the innate spark of the artist, Thea still must undergo a rebirth. Sacrificing all other endeavors and relationships, Thea's "work becomes [her] personal life." As she explains, "You are not much good until it does. It's like being woven in a big web. You can't pull away, because all your little tendrils are woven into the picture. It takes you up, and uses you, and spins you out; and that is your life. Not much else can happen to you" (546). The art and the artist become one solitary soul.

Through an allusion to Gluck's *Orfeo ed Euridice,* Cather emphasizes the transcendental power of opera. Appropriately, Thea's first piano teacher, A. Wunsch, an aging German musician, introduces her to Gluck's opera: "the most beautiful opera ever made" (89). As Wunsch's affection for Gluck's work demonstrates, opera stirs up old memories and renews deep passions. In the opera, Orpheus, a singer and poet, embodies the lyric artist. When he braves the underworld to bring his lover, Euridice, back from Elysium, his music softens the specters and furies of Hades. It even conquers the powers of death and the limits of temporal existence. Playing upon his lyre, Orpheus expresses deep grief over his lover's death, hope for her restoration, and joy at their ultimate reconciliation. His songs elicit the pity of the gods. Jupiter offers Orpheus the opportunity to descend into Hades and retrieve his lover.

> If by the sweet sound of your lyre,
> If by your charming voice,
> You can assuage the wrath
> Of the stern gods of Erebus,
> She shall return to you,
> From the dark region of Pluto
> She shall return to you. (Gluck 7)

Orpheus ultimately succeeds in regaining Euridice from the depths of Hades but only with the assistance of Love. If Wagnerian opera precipitates Thea's transformation, however, why does Cather choose Gluck's as Wunsch's ideal? Even though Italian opera reigned supreme for many decades of the 1800s (when Wunsch would have been a young man), the proscenium arch of the Metropolitan Opera House bore the inscribed names of six composers: Beethoven, Mozart, Gluck, Meyerbeer, Gounod, and Wagner. As John Dizikes observes, "The most striking thing is the absence of any Italian names; Verdi, Rossini, and Donizetti held the Metropolitan stage but were not honored above it" (239). So, Wunsch is already exhibiting a progressive opinion when he chooses *Orfeo ed Euridice* as his favorite, even though it is not a Wagnerian opera. The reign of German and Wagnerian opera at the Metropolitan (and in America) would occur several years after Wunsch taught Thea.

Wunsch recalls that "only one woman could sing [Euridice]" that well (Cather, *Song* 90). Thea seeks the source of that singer's greatness. She assumes that the woman must have been beautiful, but with deep emotion in his voice, Wunsch adamantly protests that "she was the most—*künst-ler-isch*!" (92) —the most "artistic." In that early exchange with her teacher, Thea discovers the secret of the greatest musician, the greatest artist. When Wunsch leaves Moonstone after a drunken outbreak, he gives his old, tattered score of Gluck's opera to his young and promising pupil. At the top of the title page he writes, "Einst, O Wunder!—" (120). As he offers the gift to Thea, he explains that "in ten years she would either know what the inscription meant, or she would not have the least idea, in which case it would not matter" (120). Years later, while studying in Harsanyi's piano studio, Thea hears her teacher sing those inscripted words—the lyrics to a composition by Beethoven, *Adelaide*, op. 46. Set to music by Beethoven, the words of Friedrich von Matthisson's poem "Adelaide" speak of the power of memory and love. Borrowing the first phrase of the fourth stanza of the poem for his inscription, "Once, O Miracle!" Wunsch has expressed the hopes and affections he has for Thea. Even his last name, Wunsch, suggests his "desire" to instill a love of music and a driving ambition in his pupil. He recognizes the great artist in Thea, even when she is still a child. Yet, he also knows that she must claim that identity for herself.

Years later, as a piano student in Chicago, Thea sings the aria from *Orfeo ed Euridice* for her new teacher, Harsanyi. As she sings, Harsanyi recognizes her aptitude and artistry. Exploring her range, her breathing techniques, and her style, he concludes that "she [sings] from the bottom of herself" (237). Convinced that Thea is "very talented" and has a "remarkable voice" (256), Harsanyi believes that she has a "vocation for the voice, not for the piano" (263). At his urging, she begins to explore her voice through proper training. Not coincidentally, the man that Harsanyi consults for advice about voice teachers is Theodore Thomas, the conductor of the Chicago Symphony Orchestra. Described by historian John Dizikes as "the most influential Wagnerian advocate of the 1870s" (237), the German-born Thomas introduced many Americans to Wagner's music through his concerts. The founder of the Chicago Symphony, Thomas also established the American Opera Company to produce "American opera," which he defined as "opera in English performed by American casts" (Eisler 125). Thomas leased the Academy of Music in New York for his productions, and the first season was launched on January 4, 1886. His goal, Thomas stated, was "to establish a standard for opera in this country" (126). Ironically, in Cather's novel, Thomas recalls his own awakening out of "adolescent drowsiness" by "two voices, by two women who sang in New York in 1851—Jenny Lind and Henrietta Sontag" (*Song* 259). According to the narrator, "They were the first great artists he had ever heard, and he never forgot his debt to them" (259). While Thomas would be remembered as the champion of Wagnerian music, Cather's Thomas recalls that Lind and Sontag "gave me my first feeling for the Italian style" (260). By including these historical figures in her novel, Cather situates the narrative during a time of transformation for American opera. As Thea awakens to her own artistic voice, American opera awakens to a new composer and a new artistic ideal.

Shortly after Harsanyi discovers Thea's talent for singing, he gives her a ticket to the symphony. The orchestra opens with the "Entry of the Gods into Walhalla" from Wagner's opera, *Rhinegold*. Hearing Wagner's music stirs Thea to an epiphany. She claims her artistic identity and her womanhood in that instant. The narrator explains this Wagnerian transformation: "As long as she lived that ecstasy was going to be hers. She would live for it, work for it, die for it; but she was going to have it, time after time, height after height. She could hear the crash of the orchestra again, and she rose on the brasses. She would have it, what the trumpets were singing! She would have it, have it—it! Under the old cape she pressed her hands upon her heaving bosom, that was a little girl's no longer" (254–55). Indeed, Thea eventually comes to possess the Wagner operas. She embodies Elizabeth (*Tannhäuser*), Elsa (*Lohengrin*), Venus (*Tannhäuser*), Fricka (*Rhinegold*), and Sieglinde (*Die Walküre*). As a consummate artist, she reinvents and reinterprets each of these roles, making them her own. Sherrill Harbison notes that these operas reveal "the secret of Wagner's power" (31)--the ability to deliver sensuality and spirituality in the same work. She explains that "straight-laced Victorians listening to the long, unclimaxed raptures of *Tristan's Liebestod*, to the thrusting Venusberg theme in *Tannhäuser*, or to Siegmund and Sieglinde's incestuous melting into the spring night in *Die Walküre* found themselves both aroused and frustrated [. . .]" (151). Embodying these roles, Thea discovered the simultaneous melding of eroticism and aestheticism.

In Thea's debut role in Dresden, she portrays Elizabeth in *Tannhäuser.*[3] In Act 2, scene 1 of the opera, Elizabeth heralds the "hall of song." She sings: "O hall of song I give thee greeting! / All hail to thee thou hallowed place!" (*Authentic Librettos* 40). Thea's debut role marks her entrance into the world of song and artistry. In Part 5 of the novel, "Kronborg," Thea's rebirth as a diva is complete. Through other characters' responses to Thea, Cather builds a definition of the consummate artist. With body and voice working together, Thea ensures that "every movement was the right movement, that her body was absolutely the instrument of her idea" (*Song* 571). That idea, the musical idea, informed Thea's interpretation. Rather than merely singing the notes on the page, she focused on the "basic idea, pulsing behind every bar [. . .]. She simplifies a character down to the musical idea it's built on, and makes everything conform to that" (511). By focusing not only on the music but also on the power of the myth behind it, Thea recognizes that "artistic growth is, more than anything else, a refining of the sense of truthfulness" (571). Only Thea's teacher, Harsanyi, recognizes her "secret." "Her secret? It is every artist's secret," he explains, "passion. That is all" (570). Harsanyi understands that only the true artist transforms that passion into an idea that expresses itself through the medium of her art. As Thea Kronborg demonstrates, the mind, the voice, and the body of the artist must work in harmony.

Fred Ottenburg, Thea's lover and fellow musician, describes the essence and power of her voice: "There's the voice itself, so beautiful and individual, and then there's something else; the thing in it which responds to every shade of thought and feeling, spontaneously, almost unconsciously" (509).

The ideal medium for an artist's expression, according to Cather, is Wagnerian opera. As Giannone explains, in opera "myth holds the old human stories; music the old feelings" (89). In the novel's climactic scene, Thea finally receives the opportunity to portray the coveted role of Sieglinde from *Die Walküre*, the second opera of Wagner's epic *Ring* cycle. As she vowed in the Chicago Symphony Hall, Thea claims the ecstasy of Wagner's dramatic epic as her own. Bringing together representative figures in the audience from all the stages of Thea's life, Cather creates an eroticized moment in the Metropolitan Opera House the night "Kronborg" portrays Sieglinde. With Ottenburg and Doctor Archie seated in the orchestra circle, Harsanyi in box seats near the stage, and Spanish Johnny, the old Mexican from Moonstone, in the top gallery, Thea Kronborg triumphantly embodies the preeminent artist. "At last," exclaims Harsanyi, "somebody with *enough*! Enough voice and talent and beauty, enough physical power. And such a noble, noble style" (569). Though her art has demanded a sacrifice of everything else, Thea gives "much noble pleasure to a world that needs all it can get [. . .]" (578). Through Thea's illustrative life, Cather exclaims that the artist's calling is noble—almost divine.

Almost two decades before Cather published *The Song of the Lark* (1915) or interviewed Louise Homer, Geraldine Farrar, and Olive Fremstad for "Three American Singers" (1913), she contemplated the cost for the female artist of pursuing art. According to Cather, the female artist drives "beyond herself until she is greater than she knows or means to be" (*Collected Fiction* 408). Three of Cather's stories written from 1897 to 1900 illustrate her keen awareness of the perils of artistic success—even at the beginning of her career. In these earliest portrayals, Cather chooses the diva to represent the female artist, and she suggests that the artist's life exacts the highest toll from women.

In their 1913 interview for *McClure's Magazine*, American diva Geraldine Farrar told Cather that "she does not believe that conjugal and maternal duties are easily compatible with artistic development; she does not believe that, for an artist, anything can be very real or very important except art" (36). Sixteen years before the interview with Farrar, one of Cather's characters makes the same assertion. Madame Traduttori, the aging diva in "Nanette: An Aside" (1897), explains that "when I began life, between me and this [opera career] lay everything dear in life—every love, every human hope. I have had to bury what lay between" (*Collected Fiction* 410). In "Nanette" and in a reworking of essentially the same plot, "A Singer's Romance" (1900), Cather asserts that the artist's existence is a solitary one, devoid of meaningful romantic relationships. Despite the suggestion of the story's title, the diva of "A Singer's Romance," Selma Schumann, "was a singer without a romance. No one felt the incongruity of this more than she did, yet she had lived to the age of two-and-forty without ever having known an *affair de coeur*" (336). Even though the careers of Tradutorri and Schumann "seem[ed] so gay to the uninitiated," each of the divas "had wished for a romance" (337). Their romantic dreams of love and domestic happiness, however, are sacrificed to a higher calling: art.

Art's paradoxical nature—at once eternal and fleeting—reinforces for Cather both its authenticity and the necessary sacrifice of the artist. The human voice perfectly embodies the artistic persona; it exhibits great beauty and fragility. In a 1926 interview published in *The Writer* magazine, John Chapin Mosher comments upon the importance of this dichotomy in Cather's fiction. "It was the effort their [great singers] ambition and their genius forced upon them that was significant to her, rather than their beauty and romance" (Bohlke 94). The singer's struggle to breathe life into her art exacted all the creativity and passion she could muster. Art possessed her time, her energy, and her affections, consuming her very existence. While achieving a degree of immortality through her art, the diva had to face the eventual loss not only of her youth but also of her voice—the vehicle of her art.

In "The Prodigies" (1897) Cather offers a compelling illustration of the fragility of the artist's "voice"—the mode of communicating her art to her audience. Mrs. Mackenzie, a former piano virtuoso, acknowledges that "if the cruelly exacting life of art is not wholly denied a woman, it is offered to her at a terrible price" (413). Demanding a sacrifice of body and soul, the true artist must be willing to devote all of her life force to the pursuit of beauty in art. The prodigies referred to in Cather's title are siblings—Hermann and Adrienne Massey—who demonstrate a remarkable talent for singing. Basking in the glory of their talent, their mother relentlessly orchestrates a musical career for the two. Mrs. Massey claims that "in their art they cannot begin too soon. It is the work of a lifetime, you know, a lifelong consecration" (418). Rather than choosing the artist's life, however, these children are compelled by an overly ambitious mother to pursue a rigorous schedule of lessons and concerts. Ironically, as the brother and sister perform the parting duet from *Juliette,* singing of the "immeasurable anguish of that farewell" (418), Adrienne collapses. The doctor's assessment illustrates the tenuous nature both of the human voice and of human life: "Your [Mrs. Massey's] foreign teachers have not been content with duping you out of your money, they have simply drained your child's life out of her veins" (422). Adrienne Massey's fate confirms that the artist's life must not be entered into lightly or by compulsion.

Cather collected four more stories featuring opera divas in *Youth and the Bright Medusa* (1920): "The Diamond Mine" (1916), "A Gold Slipper" (1917), "Scandal" (1919), and "Coming, Aphrodite!" (1920). All of these stories were published after *Song of the Lark* (1915), suggesting that Cather was still wrestling with the artist's fate, despite her definitive portrayal of Thea Kronborg's Wagnerian transcendence through art. The stories in *Youth and the Bright Medusa* explore the competing pressures of art and commodification. As an object of public consumption, the diva surrenders to the public onstage, but she soon discovers that its insatiable appetite cannot be satisfied during her performances. Although clearly at odds with the pursuit of real art, the public market and the media prove exacting taskmasters for the singers.

When P. T. Barnum orchestrated Jenny Lind's American tour in 1850, he introduced the machinery of diva stardom. He carefully planned and publicized her tour, crafting the myth of the "Swedish Nightingale." With careful marketing by Barnum, Lind sold herself to the American public not only as a great singer but also as a woman of pristine character: "She never traveled on the Sabbath and her charities eventually became as famous as her singing," earning her a "saintly persona" (Davis 34). Ironically, when Jenny Lind took a husband in Boston in 1852, the public felt cheated. With Lind's marriage, her fans could no longer entertain the fantasy of the "chaste goddess of the North" (Davis 35). Although Lind's tour occurred before Cather's birth, its influence was legendary. Barnum recognized the power of the public, and subsequent performers learned to appreciate the power of publicity.

All of Cather's stories featuring opera divas demonstrate a heightened awareness of the devastating effects of the promotional machinery of the public market. "Scandal" offers the clearest illustration. Kitty Ayrshire, the diva of "Scandal" (1919), learns that she is the possession of the public, and, therefore, of publicity. Publicity simultaneously promotes her career and fabricates the details of her personal life. Even though she is a victim of rumor and gossip, she learns that the intrigue her public image creates propels her fame on the stage. As the story opens, Kitty Ayrshire is recovering from a "persistent inflammation of the vocal cords which defied the throat specialist" and kept her from appearing at the opera "for nearly two months" (Cather, *Youth* 151). Her illness "gave rise to rumours—rumours that she had lost her voice, that at some time last summer she must have lost her discretion" (152). These false speculations trouble Kitty, for "she wished to believe that everything for sale in *Vanity Fair* was worth the advertised price. When she ceased to believe in these delights, she told herself, her pulling power would decline and she would go to pieces" (153). She tells her friend Pierce Tevis that "everything has been shut out from me but—gossip. That always gets in. Often I don't mind, but this time I have. People do tell such lies about me" (159).

But Tevis realizes the power of the public appetite: "Of course we [the public] do. That's part of our fun, one of the many pleasures you give us. It only shows how hard up we are for interesting public personages; for a royal family, for romantic fiction, if you will" (159). Tevis insists that it is Ayrshire's "singular good luck" that she is the "sort of person who makes myths" (159). As he explains, "A whole staff of publicity men, working day and night, couldn't do for you what you do for yourself. There is an affinity between you and the popular imagination" (160). Kitty, however, longs to remove herself from the constraints of the legend that has been created around her. She complains, "I'm getting almost as tired of the person I'm supposed to be as of the person I really am. I wish you would invent a new Kitty Ayrshire for me, Pierce. Can't I do something revolutionary? Marry, for instance?" (160). At the mere suggestion that she could control her own image, Tevis revolts. He warns the diva: "Whatever you do, don't try to change your legend. You have now the one that gives the greatest satisfaction to the greatest number of people. Don't disappoint your public" (160). "Your public," Tevis argues, "gives you what is best for you. Let well enough alone" (160). The public's "popular imagination," however, "for some reason wished [Ayrshire] to have a son" (160), so it gave her one—even though his existence was a fabrication. Ultimately, Ayrshire comes to a melancholy conclusion: "What's the use of discretion?" (177). She learns that the public worships a talent for artistry, but it also craves a marketable image that it can craft, contort, and consume.

In an attempt to craft an image the public would find more palatable, many opera singers adopted a new name to use when performing. Cather demonstrates her awareness of this trend when she discusses the creation of the character Eden Bower in "Coming, Aphrodite!" Born Edna Bowers, Eden adapts her name in an effort to appeal to her public. She willingly submits herself to the advice of her career promoters, even when that requires taking on a new identity. Several of the most prominent and successful singers during Cather's era had changed their names to facilitate their debuts, and, ultimately, their careers. Born Marie Louise Cécile Emma Lajeunesse on November 1, 1847, the Canadian soprano later changed her surname to Albani. Davis explains that "her Italian elocution master, a Signor Delorenzi, suggested Albani, the name of an old Italian family whose members, with the exception of an aged cardinal, were all dead" (83). Evidently, New York audiences preferred for their divas to possess "the exotic foreign touch" (Davis 83). Similarly, the American soprano Lillian Nordica adopted that surname because her Italian voice teacher, Sangiovanni, convinced her that her legal surname, Norton, would not be acceptable in Italy. Sangiovanni suggested "the more euphonious-sounding Giglio Nordica, and it was as 'the Lily of the North' that Lillian made her professional debut in opera" (132). Cather loosely bases the character Cressida Garnet from "The Diamond Mine" on Lillian Nordica. Not surprisingly, Garnet willingly offers herself to a consuming public in order to promote her own success. The story opens with a description of Garnet "good naturedly posing" for "young men with cameras" (67). "She was much too an American not to believe in publicity," the narrator reports. If the public pressured female performers to recreate their own identities by adopting new names, what else would they demand?

Cather recognized that another form of public consumption proved even more damaging for the female artist. In *The Diva's Mouth: Body, Voice, and Prima Donna Politics,* Susan Leonardi and Rebecca Pope suggest that "divahood" demands that a singer's "body be both object and agent/subject. While it is her voice and her body that make the sounds, that create the art, they are also the things heard and looked at" (96). Throughout "Coming, Aphrodite!" (1920) Cather simultaneously focuses the reader's attention on the body and the voice of the young diva, Eden Bower. Eden's "voice, like her figure, inspired respect" (Cather, *Youth* 13). The singer's neighbor, an aspiring painter named Don Hedger, particularly admires her queenly person. Before Bower and Hedger meet, he secretly watches her through a knothole inside his closet. He makes this discovery quite accidentally: "When he took his overcoat from its place against the partition, a long ray of yellow light shot across the dark enclosure,—a knot hole, evidently, in the high wainscoting of the west room. He had never noticed it before, and without realizing what he was doing, he stopped and squinted through it" (16). The vision that awaits him on the other side is Eden's "wholly unclad" body. "Nudity was not improper to anyone who had worked so much from the figure," but Hedger "had never seen a woman's body so beautiful as this one" (17). Hedger's fascination with Eden exists apart from her vocal talent. For him, "she had no geographical associations; unless with Crete, or Alexandria, or Veronese's Venice. She was the immortal conception, the perennial theme" (22). After Eden moves out of the apartment adjoining Hedger's, he returns to his closet and "kne[els] down before the wall" where he discovers that "the knot hole had been plugged up with a ball of wet paper,—the same blue notepaper" on which her farewell letter was written (59). Eden has known that Hedger watched her all along. "She casually accepts the voyeurism of her artist neighbor [. . .] because she knows that her life will be a public one and her body her public instrument" (96), suggest Leonardi and Pope. Cather recognizes that the female artist must confront the public's assumption that she is on display for the consumption and pleasure of her audience. As Eden Bower demonstrates, however, some female artists felt compelled to acquiesce in the subject's position in order to achieve "success."

Like Eden Bower, Kitty Ayrshire, the diva in "A Gold Slipper" (1917), finds her body objectified by her admirers; however, unlike Eden, she understands the distinction between empty bodily appetites and true artistic passion. Kitty Ayrshire defies all of Marshall McKann's expectations of "the artist." Although he, a business man, "comfortably classed all singers—especially operatic singers—as 'fat Dutchwomen' or 'shifty Sadies,' [. . .] Kitty would not fit into his clever generalization" (128). Instead, she "displayed, under his nose, the only kind of figure he considered worth looking at—that of a very young girl, supple and sinuous and quick-silverish; thin, eager shoulders, polished white arms that were nowhere too fat and nowhere too thin" (34). Kitty understands that "she could only satisfy [the craving for the divine ideal] by starving all the other hungers" (141) in her life. While the reader might expect Kitty to rebuke McKann for objectifying her body, she attempts to redirect his passion. Without passion, one can never experience the divine ideal, art, which reveals itself as a passionate craving—even if it is at variance with the desires of the flesh. As an artist, Kitty gives "to the really gifted ones, my wish, my desire, my light," a sacrifice she equates with "giving one's blood!" (141). She encourages McKann to understand the meaning of art as "a divine ideal [that] was disclosed to us, directly at variance with our appetites"; and one often feels in art those very appetites that have been denied. The ache they cause "is even the subject of the greatest of all operas" (141), Kitty comments. Cather does not allow this diva to remain objectified in the subject's position; instead, she asserts her agency as a participant in a divine ideal: art.

Cather was also aware of the dangers of material success for a great female singer. The title of Cather's "The Diamond Mine" (1916) suggests her theme. Viewing the career of Cressida Garnet, a middle-aged diva, as a "golden stream," family and friends "regarded her as a natural source of wealth; a copper vein, a diamond mine" (Cather, *Youth* 119). Believing that they are entitled to a share of her possessions, her siblings, spouses, and son never seem to recognize that the "golden stream" of her success "came out of the industry, out of the mortal body of a woman" (119). Instead, they treat Garnet as an expendable asset. Like any other commodity offered in a capitalistic market, Cressida Garnet "appealed to the acquisitive instinct in men" (81), sentencing her to a series of unfortunate marriages.

Cather found her inspiration for Cressida Garnet in Lillian Nordica, the American soprano, who could sing it all, "from the coloratura fireworks of Mozart's Queen of the Night, through the lyrical refinement of Verdi's Gilda and Gounod's Marguerite, to the vocal drama of Meyerbeer's Sélika and Wagner's Kundry" (Davis 129). Like Cather's character, Nordica married several times, and happiness eluded her each time. As historian Peter Davis records, Nordica confessed in a letter to her sister that she had been "duped, betrayed, deceived, and abused" (143) by the men in her life. The diva's third husband, George Washington Young, was a New Jersey banker and corporation director. Although considered wealthy at the time of his marriage to Nordica, he lost millions of dollars in the stock market and resorted to "gradually replacing the precious stones in her diamond tiaras with paste" (Davis 143). He found a literal "diamond mine" in his diva-wife, and he pillaged her fortune. Young did not fail to recognize himself in Cather's fictitious portrayal of Cressida Garnet's fourth husband, Jerome Brown, a Wall Street financier who squandered his wife's money to save his failed investment schemes. Still living when Cather wrote "A Diamond Mine," George Young found Cather's thinly disguised version of himself extremely unsavory. In letters to H. L. Mencken and to Ferris Greenslet in 1916 (Stout, *Calendar* 57, 59) Cather mentions Young's objections to the story and his threats to sue.[4] The consumption of the female artist was an ugly reality that Cather's fiction illuminated.

Despite the perils of commodification and public consumption, Cather ultimately maintained the hope that art could overcome any adversity that the artist encountered. Two years prior to the publication of *Youth and the Bright Medusa,* Cather wrote a letter to Greenslet, who served as the associate editor for the *Atlantic Monthly* from 1902 to 1907 and then as the literary editor at Houghton Mifflin for thirty-five years, asking him if he wanted a volume of stories about musicians and singers. In the letter, she proposed including "The Diamond Mine," "The Gold Slipper," and some new stories, too (Stout, *Calendar* 68).

Although the collection that actually followed in 1920 (*Youth and the Bright Medusa*) does not focus exclusively on singers, it continues the tradition of *The Troll Garden* (1905) by reflecting upon the nature of art and the artist. In *Willa Cather: The Writer and Her World*, Janis Stout suggests that these stories are "actually a subset of a group of stories about women's work and careers more generally, written during the years when Cather was redefining her own vocation." Stout notes that "during these same years the Great War was causing dramatic changes in women's work lives throughout America and elsewhere." She rejects the suggestion that Cather was "turning aside from real-world issues to a rarified aestheticism" (130). But Cather's strategy should not be reduced to an either-or choice between the two. She knew from personal experience (and from other real-life examples like Lillian Nordica) that the female artist confronted significant challenges, despite the continuing inroads being made by the women's movement. However, rather than suggesting that the cost of pursuing art is futile, Cather embraced the exacting profession. For her, the possibilities of artistic transcendence outweighed all the necessary sacrifices and dangers.

As *The Song of the Lark* demonstrates, Cather, like Wagner, believed that the artist carried the burden of articulating the "two cardinal needs of humanity": "a religious chant" and an "art song" (Cather, *World* 2: 645). In her interview with Cather, Geraldine Farrar echoed the author's own artistic philosophy. As Cather recalls, Farrar "quot[ed] with fervor that there is nothing in the world so ugly that it can not be made beautiful in art; and that there is nothing in the world so beautiful that it can not be made banal by a stupid or prudish artist" (Cather, "Three American Singers" 38). The conclusion of *The Song of the Lark* reaffirms Cather's faith in the transcendent power of art and in the high calling of the artist. "Artistic growth is, more than it is anything else, a refining of the sense of truthfulness," the narrator asserts. "The stupid believe that to be truthful is easy; only the artist, the great artist, knows how difficult it is" (571).

4

A STANDARD OF TASTE AND FORM

Opera in the Cosmopolitan World of James and Wharton

During the latter half of the nineteenth century, the entire social structure in America's industrial capitals shifted. From the end of the Civil War to the turn of the century, an explosion of new wealth occurred as entrepreneurs in industry, railroading, and mining quickly accumulated vast fortunes. Although their wealth enabled these newly minted millionaires to indulge in vulgar displays of capital through their purchases of property and possessions, it did not guarantee entry into the inner circle of America's aristocracy. Despite the efforts of the old guard, however, the nouveaux riches eventually pushed their way into the ranks of society, fundamentally altering the balance of power in the social and market economies.

New York society exemplified this turn-of-the-century transformation. Frederic Jaher offers the perspective of the old guard aristocrats in "Style and Status: High Society in Late-Nineteenth Century New York": "Their self-contained world of opera at the Academy of Music and quiet evenings in lower Manhattan brownstones differed greatly from the social swirl in Mrs. Astor's circle further uptown. Inherited social status, worship of the past, smaller fortunes, an anonymous, modest lifestyle, and contempt and envy for the nouveaux riches who eclipsed them defined their set of values and attitudes. For the knickerbockers, fashionable society was no longer polite society" (269–70). Unconstrained by the traditions of lineage or class, the "Invaders" instated a new measure of influence in New York—wealth.[1] In order to assert their entitlement to their elevated position, these newly minted "aristocrats" sought ways to consume and to display their wealth. In his *Theory of the Leisure Class*, Thorstein Veblen explained this cultural shift: "The subsequent relative decline in the use of conspicuous leisure as a basis of repute is due partly to an increasing relative effectiveness of consumption as an evidence of wealth [. . .]" (75). While the industrial tycoons hailed the change in cultural customs as progress, many of the intellectuals belonging to the leisured class mourned the loss of a society of manners. Veblen describes the source of such sentiments. "From the days of the Greek philosophers to the present, a degree of leisure and of exemption from contact with such industrial processes as serve the immediate everyday purposes of human life has ever been recognized by thoughtful men as a prerequisite to a worthy or beautiful, or even a blameless, human life. In itself and in its consequences the life of leisure is beautiful and ennobling in all civilized men's eyes" (42). Rather than concentrating its efforts on the customs of the respectable, the new set focused its efforts on displaying the fashionable.

Born into New York's inner circle, Henry James and Edith Wharton possessed firsthand knowledge of the cultural shifts occurring in the late nineteenth century. "James and Wharton shared the same early scene," Millicent Bell relates. "It was that 'Old New York' whose focus lay between Washington Square, where he [James] had been born in 1843, and Twenty-third Street, a mile further uptown, where she was born nearly twenty years later. Boundaries social as well as geographic defined this polite nineteenth-century Manhattan, and gave it a 'family-party smallness' as James described it, in which everyone was connected with everyone else by family recognitions and habits of association inherited for several generations" (Bell 46). Although James and Wharton would eventually leave behind the American world of their birth for Europe, they managed to "reconstruct—archeologically as it were—the social world of [their youth]: the traditions which vitalized the culture of Old New York in the period from about 1840–1880" (Tuttleton 124). Unquestionably, these expatriate writers possessed a certain amount of ambivalence about their privileged origins; however, in their fiction they "memorialize[ed] a set of slowly evolved cultural values [that had been] destroyed by a succession of disastrous changes in American life beginning in the 1880s—including the rise of the industrial plutocracy (the 'lords of Pittsburgh,' as [Wharton] so sarcastically called them); the massive immigration, which totally altered the ethnic character of New York City; [and] World War I [. . .]"

(Tuttleton 124). In *A Backward Glance,* Edith Wharton describes Henry James's expatriation (and, implicitly, her own) in these terms: "The truth is that he belonged irrevocably to the old America out of which I also came, and of which—almost—it might paradoxically be said that to follow up its last traces one had to come to Europe [. . .]" (175).

By chronicling the intricacies of the ceremonial gestures and manners of the leisure class with which they were intimately acquainted, Wharton and James offered Americans, and the world, a glimpse of a dying culture. Some of their contemporary critics derisively labeled the two as novelists of manners, but Wharton did not resist the label. Instead, she insisted that it defined the only worthwhile subject for the American novel. In "The Great American Novel," published in the *Yale Review* in 1927, Wharton wrote:

> But what does "human nature" thus denuded [of the social order] consist in, and how much of it is left when it is separated from the web of custom, manners, culture it has elaborately spun about itself? Only that hollow unreality, "Man," an evocation of the eighteenth-century demagogues who were the first inventors of "standardization." As to real men, unequal, unmanageable, and unlike each other, they are all bound up with the effects of climate, soil, laws, religion, wealth—and, above all, leisure. Leisure, itself the creation of wealth, is incessantly engaged in transmuting wealth into beauty by secreting the surplus energy which flowers in great architecture, great painting, and great literature. Only in the atmosphere thus engendered floats that impalpable dust of ideas which is the real culture. A colony of ants or bees will never create a Parthenon. (*Backward Glance* 155–56)

With the loss of the leisured class, Wharton and James noticed a vulgarity of manners and a cultural void. "Traditional society, with its old-established distinctions of class, its pass-words, exclusions, delicate shades of language and behavior, is one of man's oldest works of art, the least conscious and the most instinctive," Wharton asserts; "yet the modern American novelist is told that the social and educated being is an unreality unworthy of his attention, and that only the man with the dinner-pail is human, and hence available for his purpose" (Wharton, *Backward Glance* 155).

Like Wharton, Henry James found himself at variance with the changes occurring in America's upper crust. For him, the intrusion of Wall Street into his Washington Square world left him feeling alienated from the America of his youth. In her memoir Wharton recalls:

> Henry James was essentially a novelist of manners, and the manners he was qualified by nature and situation to observe were those of the little vanishing group of people among whom he had grown up, or their more picturesque prototypes in older societies. For better or worse he had to seek that food where he could find it, for it was the only food his imagination could fully assimilate. He was acutely conscious of this limitation, and often bewailed to me his total inability to use the "material," financial, and industrial, of modern American life. Wall Street, and everything connected with the business world, remained an impenetrable mystery to him, and knowing this he felt he could never have dealt fully in fiction with the "American scene," and always frankly acknowledged it. (*Backward Glance*, 176)

Despite his own discomfort with the "American scene," James, on at least two separate occasions, encouraged Wharton to continue pursuing the "American subject." In a letter dated October 26, 1900, James writes, "And I applaud, I mean I value, I egg you on in, your study of the American life that surrounds you." He continues his advice to Wharton: "Let yourself go in it & *at* it—it's an untouched field, really: the folk who try, over there, don't come within miles of any civilized, however superficially, any 'evolved' life. And use to the full your ironic and satiric gifts; they form a most valuable (I hold) & beneficent engine" (James and Wharton, *Letters*, 32).

Two years later, he would reiterate his encouragement of Wharton's American subjects in a letter dated August 17, 1902:

> There it [the American subject] is round you. Don't pass it by—the immediate, the real, the ours, the yours, the novelist's that it waits for. Take hold of it & keep hold, & let it pull you where it

> will. It will pull harder than things of more tarabiscotage, which is a merit in itself. Profit, be warned, by my awful example of exile & ignorance. You will say that j'en parle à mon aise—but I shall have paid for my ease, & I don't want you to pay (as much) for yours. But these are impertinent importunities—from the moment they are not developed. All the same DO NEW YORK! The 1st-hand account is precious. (James and Wharton, *Letters*, 34)

Wharton would "do New York" as no other writer of her time could. Guided by the hand of a thoughtful observer, Wharton's fiction captured the manners and customs of an age of transition. Yet, her accounts are tempered by critiques of the early "age of innocence" and the one that replaced it at the dawning of the twentieth century.

Gradually, a society ruled by conspicuous leisure was replaced by one that asserted its entitlement through conspicuous consumption. In opera, James and Wharton discovered a social institution that illustrated both the customs of the old guard and the consumption of the new wealth. James and Wharton were intimately familiar with opera and its architecture. Their diaries and letters include accounts of various performances and performers they witnessed in the United States and abroad. While the range of operatic references in their fiction is wide and varied, this study focuses on scenes that occur in the opera boxes.[2] Opera's spaces, rather than its content or its players, occupy the most important role in the novels. Quite fittingly, the changing dynamics of the "architecture of manners" (Sarah Luria's term) is reflected in the interior architecture of opera houses.

Interested in the parallels between internal and external "spaces," Ulfried Reichardt notes: "If the public is understood as a market, persons offer their characteristic features like a commodity and compete as to who is most successful. The reorganization of the structure of personality can thus be understood also as an adaptation to a changing social reality and to a changing social space" (345). Within the confines of the opera box, elaborate rituals of social privilege and rejection occurred. Box seats allowed their owners to display their wealth while simultaneously offering themselves to the public as a spectacle. In the opera box, questions of class and breeding were easily sorted out by the exclusivity of the limited space. Bruce McConachie describes the development of the elaborate social ritual of opera going:

> Between 1825 and 1850 elite New Yorkers and their allies in the theater developed three overlapping social conventions that gradually wrapped operagoing in a mantle of mystery. The first and most important of these was separating opera from theater by establishing a special place for its performance. During the same decades, fashionable Gothamites also worked to sharpen and objectify a code of behavior, including a dress code, deemed proper when attending the opera. Finally, upper-class New Yorkers increasingly insisted that only foreign-language opera could meet their standards of excellence—standards upheld by behavior and criticism employing foreign words and specialized language impenetrable to all but the cognoscenti. (182)

Nineteenth-century etiquette books for ladies included detailed descriptions of appropriate attire and behavior at the opera. Florence Hartley's *The Ladies' Book of Etiquette, and Manual of Politeness: A Complete Handbook for the Use of the Lady in Polite Society* includes an entire section on "The Opera." It begins with the following admonition to all ladies: "Here you should wear full dress, an opera cloak, and either a headdress, or dressy bonnet of some thin material. Your gloves must be of kid, white, or some very light tint to suit your dress. Many dress for the opera, as they would for the theatre; but the beauty of the house is much enhanced by each lady contributing her full dress toilette to the general effect" (174). According to the manual's language, the women provide a living adornment to the already gilded interior spaces of the opera house.

As numerous critics have observed, James's fiction is often told in language that alludes to an observer or spectator. References to eyes and verbs of vision reveal the writer's interest in this theme. Jean-Christophe Agnew argues that James's "early aesthetic awakenings" are intimately linked to "the peculiarly active and powerful strain of inflection James gives to the word 'spectatorship.' " According to Agnew, James's vision, "in an almost physical sense, 'takes in' the world; takes it in so as not to be taken in by it. He describes his youthful hunger for impressions as a 'visionary ache,' and speaks of this ache as a 'dark difficulty at which one could but secretly stare—secretly because one was somehow ashamed of its being there and would have quickly removed one's eyes, or tried to clear them, if caught in the act of watching' " (81).

James's perceptive gaze was always searching for the ideal lens to filter his insights. Possessing the aesthete's sensibility, James believed that the artist rendered a unique perspective. It is not surprising that James would choose the opera as a locus for the exploration of perception. Although he referred to himself as a "non-musical auditor" (qtd. in Tintner, *Cosmopolitan World* 282), James attended numerous performances in American and European opera houses. These experiences were absorbed into his fiction. "When James brought an opera actively into a novel or story, he was attracted by the spectacle of the opera house itself as well as by the music that was played," Tintner explains. In "Eugene Pickering" (1874), *The American* (1877), *The Portrait of a Lady* (1881), and "A London Life" (1888), James uses the opera box to explore the relationship between perception and deception—a theme that would culminate in "Glasses" (1896), a short story influenced by Poe's "The Spectacles." In addition, these opera box scenes,[3] much like Wharton's, reveal the forms, tastes, and codes of the elite.

In "Eugene Pickering," James's first story that employs opera as a setting, vision is a central concern. Young Eugene Pickering eventually learns the painful and disillusioning lesson that appearances and reality are not always the same. Filled with the language of vision, the story focuses the reader's attention on Pickering's perception. The opera box scene allows the narrator and the reader (as spectators) to eavesdrop on the initial deployment of the deception that destroys Pickering's innocence. James subtly prepares the way to the box by including a telling motif—opera glasses. After his overprotective father's death, Eugene Pickering discovers that "life offered itself to [him] for the first time" (*Complete* 3 :309), and the young American travels to Europe for a six-month tour. Even after he reached adulthood, Pickering's father "kept an opera-glass at hand, and when [Eugene] was out in the garden he used to watch [him] with it" (308). With his freedom stifled in this way, Pickering longs to go "everywhere" and see "everything"

(309). After six weeks of traveling independently in Europe, Pickering believes that now his "eyes are open," and he is filled with a "feverish sense of liberation" (310). By the story's conclusion, however, Pickering falls victim to his own vision; after all, "his unworldly life had not been of a sort to sharpen his perception of the ridiculous" (321).

In constructing the opera scene, James uses Adelina Patti as a touchstone for judging tastes and forms. For James, she represented his earliest memories of opera and his youth in New York. Like Wharton, James's introduction to opera came at an early age. In *A Small Boy and Others*, James remembers hearing his elders talk of "those rich old Italian names, Bosio and Badiali, Ronconi and Steffanone," singers they heard perform during the "lifetime of the prehistoric 'Park' " (114). Even before he was allowed to accompany them to the Park, however, he "listened to that rarest of infant phenomena, Adelina Patti" (114) at Castle Garden. "She was about of our own age," James recalls; "she was one of us, even though at the same time the most prodigious of fairies, of glittering fables" (114).

Early in the story, the narrator, an estranged childhood classmate and friend of Pickering's, expresses his interest in the "advent of Adelina Patti" (321), while Pickering remains "irresponsive" and "preoccupied" by thoughts of Anastasia Blumenthal, an enchanting German widow (321). Coincidentally, the anticipated diva arrives on the Homburg stage the same night that Madame Blumenthal "reappeared," sitting near the narrator "in a box, looking extremely pretty." He recalls, however, that "Adelina Patti was singing, and after the rising of the curtain I was occupied with the stage [. . .]" (326). James invokes Patti's artistry as a counter to the spectacle and taste of Madame Blumenthal. When the narrator converses with Madame Blumenthal about the "merits of Adelina Patti's singing," the widow remarks that she "could see no charm in it; it was meager, it was trivial, it lacked soul" (333). Their difference of opinion about Patti's singing is indicative of a more fundamental disagreement between these two characters. When the diva's voice "rose wheeling like a skylark and rained down its silver notes" (333), the narrator whispers a response to the music and a challenge to Blumenthal's pronouncement: "Ah, give me that art and I'll leave you your passion!" (333).

If the narrator is not enthralled with Blumenthal's charms, however, young Pickering certainly is. "He was sitting a little behind her, leaning forward, looking over her shoulder, and listening, while she, slowly moving her fan to and fro and letting her eye wander over the house, was apparently talking of this person and that" (325). Neither Blumenthal nor Pickering attends to the performance on stage. She observes the audience while he focuses on her. Although the narrator gives himself to Patti during the performance, he, too, looks around the house during the entr'acte. Admitting an old acquaintance, Niedermeyer, to his box, the narrator feigns ignorance by turning to Madame Blumenthal's box and inquiring, "Do tell me who and what is the lady in white, with the young man sitting behind her" (326). After inspecting her with his opera glass, Niedermeyer replies that she is Madame Blumenthal, a lady with "great charm"; "yet for all that, I'm not going to speak to her; I'm not going near her box" (328). He further explains that "there is something sinister about the woman." With his final words of judgment, Niedermeyer unknowingly prepares the narrator and the reader for the story's revelation. Perceptive to Blumenthal's deceptive powers, he concludes that "her outward charm is only the mask of a dangerous discontent. Her imagination is lodged where her heart should be!" (328).

After Niedermeyer discloses Blumenthal's past, the narrator finds that "even Adelina Patti's singing, for the next half hour, but half availed to divert me from my quickened curiosity to behold Madame Blumenthal face to face" (331). Following that impulse, he visits her box during the intermission, where he was "ushered in by Pickering with zealous hospitality." On meeting Madame Blumenthal, the narrator is surprised to find that "her prettiness lost nothing on a nearer view" despite "something faded and jaded in her physiognomy" (331). As he observes, "her movements, her smile, and the tone of her voice, especially when she laughed, had an almost girlish frankness and spontaneity" (331). Madame Blumenthal's regal presence and ingenuous charm in the opera box is a ruse, however. While she continues to play the part of a respectable young widow innocently searching for companionship and intellectual stimulation, she preys upon the inexperience of Eugene Pickering. The affections of this young man flatter the thirty-four or five-year-old widow and appeal to her vanity, but she misleads him without any intentions of forming a permanent relationship. Deceived by the display of her beauty and refinement, Pickering painfully discovers her deception. He falsely believes that she has accepted his proposal, only to be finally rejected. When he ultimately recognizes his role in Madame Blumenthal's drama, Pickering blurts out: "You've been playing a part, then; you never cared for me?" (344). She retorts, "Yes; till I knew you; till I saw how far you'd go" (344). From her appearance in the opera box until the final encounter with Pickering at Wiesbaden, Madame Blumenthal plays a role. Performance in the story is not limited to the one occurring before the footlights, but the scene in the opera box establishes the complicated deception.

Three years after "Eugene Pickering," James published *The American,* which also features a pivotal scene in the opera box. Like Pickering, Christopher Newman travels to Europe for pleasure. After acquiring a fortune adequate "enough to rest awhile, to forget the confounded thing, to look about [him], to see the world, to have a good time, to improve [his] mind, and if the fancy takes [him], to marry a wife" (30), Newman settles in Paris for an extended sojourn. Invoking the language of vision, the narrator explains that it was Newman's "eyes that chiefly told his story; an eye in which innocence and experience were singularly blended. It was full of contradictory suggestions [. . .]" (18). Newman journeys to the "Old World" of Europe to find his "new world" of leisure in "people, places, art, nature, everything!" (35). His friend Mrs. Tristam reminds Newman that by the standards of patrician France, he is a "barbarian" (42), unacquainted with the "forms and ceremonies" (43) of the upper classes. With Wall Street as his only training ground, Newman uses the language of acquisition and consumption to describe his search for a suitable wife: "I want to possess, in a word, the best article in the market" (44). Newman intrudes into the carefully codified realm of French aristocracy with the values of a culture of consumption.

In Paris, Newman selects his ideal "article in the market" for a wife: the young widow Claire de Cintré, a member of the Faubourg Saint-Germain set. Unacquainted with the habits of patrician French families, Newman possesses a "tranquil unsuspectingness of the relativity of his own place in the social scale" (152), a disposition that irritates her family, the Bellegardes. James chooses the Paris Opera for one scene where Newman's status as an outsider to the Bellegarde family is underscored. As Chapter 17 opens, Newman sits alone in his box, listening to a performance of Mozart's *Don Giovanni.*

Although the novel begins "on a brilliant day in May, in the year 1868" (17), the Parisian opera house of the novel is based on the one designed by Jean-Joseph Charles Garnier and inaugurated in 1875. James recorded his initial impressions of the new Paris Opera House in a letter to the *New York Tribune* dated December 11, 1875. "The Opera is already a historical monument; it resembles in visible, sensible shape what the Empire proposed itself to be, and it forms a kind of symbol—a very favorable one—of the Empire's legacy to France. There may be differences of opinion about the beauty of the building; to my sense it is in a high degree picturesque and effective, but it is not beautiful; but no one can deny that it is superbly characteristic; that it savors of its time; that it tells the story of the society that produced it" (*Parisian Sketches* 9). James goes on to describe some of the unique architectural features of the house:

> It is nothing but gold—gold upon gold; it has been gilded till it is dark with gold. This is doubtless, from the picturesque point of view, rather a fine effect for a theater to produce. The really strong points of the Opera are the staircase and the *foyer.* The staircase is light and brilliant, though I think a trifle vulgar; and an immense affair of white marble, overlaid with pale agates and alabasters, climbing in divergent arms and crowned with a garish fresco of nymphs and muses, in imitation (of all people in the world) of Luca Giordano. If the world were ever reduced to the dominion of a single gorgeous potentate, the *foyer* would do very well for his throne room. (*Parisian Sketches* 9–10)

The impressions garnered in the Paris Opera House filtered into James's fiction. The physical spaces of the opera house, like the characters in *The American,* combine the elements of the exquisite with the vulgar.

Newman embodies these very contradictions of character. The narrator explains that the American "took a large box and invited a party of his compatriots; this was a mode of recreation to which he was much addicted" (196). For Newman, the pleasure did not come primarily from the love of opera; instead, "he liked doing things which involved his paying for people; the vulgar truth is that he enjoyed 'treating' them" (197). A few nights before, Newman invited a group to hear the Italian contralto Madame Alboni, but one of the members of his party talked "not only during the *entr'actes,* but during many of the finest portions of the performance, so that Newman had really come away with an irritated sense that Madame Alboni had a thin, shrill voice, and that her musical phrase was much garnished with a laugh of the giggling order" (197). That experience prompted him to attend the opera unaccompanied for a while.

At the conclusion of the first act of *Don Giovanni,* Newman turns in his seat to survey the house. Though his fiancée's absence from the family box signals the Bellegardes' rejection of Newman, he does not understand the silent message of this coded behavior. He spies Claire's brother, Urbain de Bellegarde, and his wife in the box. As Maud Cooke relates in her *Manual of Etiquette, or Social Forms, Manners and Customs of Correct Society,* "At the opera it is customary for ladies and gentlemen to leave their seats, and promenade in the lobbies or *foyer* of the house during the intervals between the acts" (332). Following this convention, Newman strolls the foyer where he encounters Claire's other brother, Valentin de Bellegarde. When Newman enters the box of the dowager, Madame de Bellegarde, however, he still believes his position within their family is secure. Despite this assurance, the tension between Newman and the marquis is evident. Newman asks, "What do you think of the opera?" His inquiry is met with a derisive answer: "We all know what Mozart is; our impressions don't date from this evening. Mozart is youth, freshness, brilliancy, facility—a little too great facility perhaps. But the execution is here and there deplorably rough" (200). Although he guesses that this is Newman's first experience with Mozart's opera, the marquis remarks, "You speak as if it [the opera] were a *feuilleton* in the *Figaro.* You've surely seen the opera before?" (200). Both the Marquis's question and his tone suggest his certainty about the superiority of his taste, his experience, and his musical knowledge. Although Newman appears oblivious to the encoded messages of rejection in the opera box, James uses the scene to underscore the motivations for the Bellegardes' disdain of Newman.

Newman's failure to understand the Bellegardes' sense of honor is highlighted by Valentin's actions in Mademoiselle Nioche's box. After his conversation with Newman in the lobby, Valentin returns to Mademoiselle Nioche's *baignoire* (box seat named for its bathtub shape), even though another young man, M. Stanislas Kapp of Strasbourg, already occupies the box. Valentin presents his case to Newman:

> The box is not his (M. Kapp's); Noémie came in alone and installed herself. I went and spoke to her, and in a few moments she asked me to go and get her fan from the pocket of her cloak, which the *ouvreuse* had carried off. In my absence this gentleman came in and took the chair beside Noémie in which I had been sitting. My reappearance disgusted him, and he had the grossness to show it. He came within an ace of being impertinent. I don't know who he is; he is some vulgar wretch. I can't think where she picks up such acquaintances. He has been drinking, too, but he knows what he is about. Just now, in the second act, he was unmannerly again. I shall put in another appearance for ten minutes—time enough to give him an opportunity to commit himself, if he feels inclined. I really can't let the brute suppose that he is keeping me out of the box. (205)

The obligation Valentin feels to represent honor, manners, and good breeding compels him to challenge the vulgar M. Kapp to a duel. He tells Newman that "there is no disputing about tastes. It's a matter of feeling; it's measured by one's sense of honor" (209). Bewildered with this foreign code of conduct, Newman responds, "Oh, confound your sense of honour!" (209). In Newman's economy of values, Valentin's duel over a woman he views as a "bore" (209) is a colossal waste. Refusing to "defend the theory of dueling," Valentin merely informs Newman that "it is our custom, and I think it is a good thing. [. . .] It's a remnant of a higher-tempered time; one ought to cling to it" (211). Valentin's denunciation of Kapp parallels his family's rejection of Newman. Both are rebuffed for their vulgarity. The chapter that opens in Newman's opera box, a site of "recreation" for the American, concludes with an argument in Mademoiselle Nioche's box, the battleground of patrician honor. The scene at the Paris Opera magnifies the insurmountable differences between Newman and the Bellegardes. Newman fails to understand that he, too, may be rejected merely on the principles of a code that he cannot understand. The Bellegardes' rejection of Newman culminates in the following chapter when he learns that his fiancée has "gone away" and "cannot marry" him (212–13).

In *The Portrait of a Lady,* James once again contrasts the old and new worlds of Europe and America. While most of the novel's characters are American by birth, the action unfolds in Europe, where they are living. *Portrait* traces the journey of Isabel Archer, "a young woman affronting her destiny" (8). As James explains in his "Preface to the New York Edition" (1908), the "portrait" of this young lady is constructed of many impressions. In the "house of fiction," at each window "stands a figure with a pair of eyes, or at least with a field-glass, which forms, again and again, for observation, a unique instrument, insuring to the person making use of it an impression distinct from every other" (7). The language with which James describes the house of fiction translates into terminology appropriate for the opera house: "He and his neighbours are watching the same show, but one seeing more where the other sees less, one seeing black where the other sees white, one seeing small, one sees coarse where the other sees fine" (7). The opera box offers the ideal scene for displaying James's heroine, a woman who—as a young girl—had "kindness, admiration, bonbons, bouquets, the opportunity for dancing, plenty of new dresses, the *London Spectator,* the latest publications, the music of Gounod, the poetry of Browning, the prose of George Eliot" (41–42). As the reference to Gounod demonstrates, Isabel possesses a cultivated appreciation of opera. In this novel, however, James is once again more interested in the architecture of characters within opera's spaces than he is with a particular musical work.

Chapter 28 of the novel opens with Lord Warburton, who has already been rejected by Isabel Archer, driving "to the opera with the idea of paying them [Isabel Archer and Ralph Touchett] a visit in their box after the easy Italian fashion" (253). With the exception of mentioning the composer's name—Verdi—and Ralph's condemning judgment that "the opera's very bad; the women look like laundresses and sing like peacocks" (254), the actual opera performance is ignored. Instead, the reader, along with Lord Warburton, "pursue[s] his quest" by "scanning two or three tiers of boxes" and "perceiv[es] in one of the largest of these receptacles a lady whom he easily recognized" (253–54). "Seated facing the stage and partly screened by the curtain of the box," Isabel Archer dominates the scene.

Isabel's box engages the interest of numerous "spectators" (133). Although Isabel explains to Caspar Goodwood, another suitor, "If there's a thing in the world I'm fond of, it's my personal independence" (142), she spends most of the novel pursuing freedom down the very paths that will deny it. As the box scene demonstrates, Isabel participates in the deception to which she eventually succumbs. According to Warburton, "Miss Archer had, in operatic conditions, a radiance even a slight exaltation [. . .]" (254). Staring down at the footlights below, Isabel executes her own dramatic "arts" and "felicities" (255) in the opera box. The narrator explains that "her voice had tricks of sweetness" which she "played" on Lord Warburton (255). The other occupants of the box become supporting characters in Isabel's performance. Seated beside Isabel, Gilbert Osmond orchestrates the arrangement, making himself the focus of her attention. The box scene establishes Osmond's interest in Isabel as more than friendship when he adopts the pose of her escort. Following custom, the other occupants of the box—Ralph Touchett, Miss Stackpole, and Mr. Bantling—"take advantage of the recess to enjoy the relative coolness of the lobby" (254), but Warburton senses that they are hardly missed. Even in the midst of a crowd, Isabel and Osmond isolate themselves from everyone else. As the opera box scene demonstrates, those interested in Isabel's welfare, in seeing her "go before the breeze" (161), will have to satisfy themselves by gazing at her radiant countenance from afar—as an opera spectator would from his field glass. Surrounded by the elements of aristocratic forms and customs at the opera, Isabel inhabits the world that will appear suffocating to her after her marriage to Gilbert Osmond. That night at the opera house, aristocratic traditions appear enchanting to Isabel. Later in the novel, however, she discovers that Gilbert's slavery to "forms" and "posture[s]" fills her with a "sense of darkness and suffocation" (361).

While the opera scene in *The Portrait of Lady* precedes the ultimate deception of the novel, "A London Life" culminates in an opera box at London's Covent Garden. Again as in "Eugene Pickering," James draws upon recent events to shape his scene. In the spring of 1888, the same year of the story's publication, Lillian Nordica, an American soprano, sang the role of Valentine in Meyerbeer's *Huguenots* (the opera performed in "A London Life") at Covent Garden in London (Davis 137). The opera outing materializes when "Mr. Wendover [an American visiting London] propose[s] to Mrs. Berrington that she and her sister should honour with their presence a box he had obtained for the opera three nights later—an occasion of high curiosity, the first appearance of a young American singer of whom considerable things were expected" (175). In that climactic moment, Laura Wing, the unmarried American sister of Selina Berrington, receives confirmation of her sister's infidelity and misperceives the intentions of Mr. Wendover. As usual, the customs of proper behavior figure prominently in the box scene. The violations of those practices magnify the preexisting impropriety in the story. By placing his characters in one of Covent Garden's boxes—a "little upholstered receptacle which was so public and yet so private" (*Complete* 7: 183)—James contrasts two modes of living: a life of total disregard for appearances and a life of excruciating enslavement to them.

The characters' actions demonstrate their disregard for social customs and their inability to perceive accurately. The box provides an ideal setting for dramatizing the rules of decorum and psychology. Mr. Wendover's invitation inadvertently suggests that he intends for Laura to accompany him to the opera. As Cecil B. Hartley instructs in *The Gentlemen's Book of Etiquette, and Manual of Politeness* (1875), "If it is the first time you have invited her [to accompany you to the theatre, opera, a concert, or any other public place of amusement], include her mother, sister, or some other lady in the invitation" (294). Laura, however, appears to be the only member of her party cognizant of or concerned with such appearances. At the end of the second act, Mrs. Berrington turns to Mr. Wendover and expresses her desire to visit a friend in one of the opposite boxes. Mr. Wendover's disappointment stems from concerns other than propriety. The narrator explains that "he was disappointed—even slightly wounded: he had taken some trouble to get his box and it had been no small pleasure to him to see it graced by the presence of a celebrated beauty

[Selina Berrington]. Now his situation collapsed if the celebrated beauty were going to transfer her light to another quarter" (177). Only Laura reads Selina's actions as "inconsiderate" and "rude" (177).

Selina, however, understands her breach of conduct; she simply chooses to abandon forms for her own desires. She "trie[s] to perform her act of defection in a soothing, conciliating way, so far as appealing eyebeams went; but she g[ives] no particular reason for her escapade, with[holds] the name of friends in question and betray[s] no consciousness that it is not usual for ladies to roam about the lobbies" (177). Understanding the compromising position that Selina's absence places her in, Laura "had a sense of wrong—of being made light of; for Mrs. Berrington certainly knew that honorable women didn't (for the appearance of the thing) arrange to leave their unmarried sister sitting alone, publicly, at the playhouse, with a couple of young men [. . .]" (178). After her sister abandons her, Laura feels "exhibited" to "the people in the opposite box" in a disparaging manner (179). The occupants of all the box seats participate in a spectacle of display, but the carefully codified rules of conduct attempted to dispel any vulgarity that might accompany such spectacles. When these rules were not followed, then the "myriad eyes" of the audience could make inferences.

After Selina's departure from Wendover's box, Laura becomes "more and more unaware of the music" despite the "remarkable flights" executed as the American singer "trilled and warbled" (179). Laura fears the searching gazes from the other boxes, surveying the "curtained dimness" with her opera glass, expecting to see that Selina and her lover, Captain Crispin, have met (179). Throughout the story, Laura has despaired that Selina is jeopardizing her marriage by engaging in an affair with Captain Crispin. Married to a young English aristocrat, Lionel Berrington, Selina enjoys the social position of her marriage, but she resents the duties prescribed to her as wife and mother. Without much regard for propriety, Selina flaunts her indiscretions. Her sister, recognizing the protections the Berrington marriage affords her as an unmarried woman, begs her to reform her behavior. If her sister's disregard for London's code of conduct leads to divorce, Laura, too, will find herself in the "unspeakabl[y] dreary" position of relying on distant relatives for financial security (212).

Propriety allows Laura Wing to perceive accurately her sister's motivations; however, it also misleads her in assessing Wendover's intentions, resulting in a tangled conclusion to the opera box scene. Recognizing that her reputation is on display, Laura "hesitates, looking down the curved lobby, where there was nothing to see but the little numbered doors of the boxes" (182). Alone with Mr. Wendover "in the lamplit bareness" while "the finale of the act was ringing and booming behind them" (182), Laura attempts to escape her disgrace. Mr. Wendover urges her to remain: "Do stay—what difference does it make. [. . .] And the last act is so fine" (183). Already a victim of Selina's deception, Laura mistakes Mr. Wendover's "conscious sympathy, entreaty, vindication, [and] tenderness" (183) for her as romantic affection. "Taking the most important step of her life" (183), as she later confesses to a friend, Laura desperately asks him to marry her. To her horror, she discovers that her impression of his feelings for her was erroneous. In the opera box, the competing forces of concealment and revelation are played out in a complicated drama.

As "Eugene Pickering," *The American*, *The Portrait of a Lady*, and "A London Life" demonstrate, the opera house provided James with an ideal setting for one of his most prominent themes: vision. Because the opera box represented the luxury of the upper classes, it also provided a suitable venue for displaying wealth and beauty. In "Glasses," James achieves his most complete consideration of the relationship of vision and vanity. Borrowing from Edgar Allan Poe's "The Spectacles" (1844),[4] James creates Flora Saunt, the quintessential Jamesian heroine—one who possesses an inability to see the world as it really is. She suffers from impaired vision yet refuses to embrace the disfiguring cure of spectacles. Like Poe, James recognizes that vision requires far more than the physical health of one's eyes. Every gaze involves a spectator and a subject, and James plays with these roles.

In a notebook entry dated June 26, 1895, James records his idea for "Glasses":

> A little idea occurred to me the other day for a little tale that Maupassant would have called *Les Lunettes*, though I'm afraid that *The Spectacles* won't do. A very pretty, a very beautiful little woman, devoted to her beauty, which she cherishes, prizing, and rejoicing in it more than in anything on earth—is threat-

> ened, becomes indeed absolutely afflicted, with a malady of the eyes which she goes to see oculists about. She has had it for a long time, and has been told that she must wear spectacles of a certain kind, a big strong unbecoming kind, with a *bar* across them, etc. –if she wishes to preserve her sight. (125)

With the exception of the character's gender, this sketch could describe Poe's Napoleon Buonaparte Froissart Simpson. The physical deficiency of vision, however, is not either character's primary weakness. According to James's notebook entry, his heroine "has been unable to face this disfigurement—she has evaded and defrauded the obligation (wearing them [corrective spectacles] only in secret and sometimes changing them for glasses, etc.) and she has got worse [*sic*]. She adores her beauty, and it has other adorers" (Edel and Powers 125–26). Saunt claims that "I'm happy to say there's nothing the matter with any part of my body; not the least little thing! [. . .] I've good teeth, a good digestion, and a good temper. I'm sound of wind and limb!" (James, *Embarrassments* 103). Unable to "submit to the imputation of a flaw," Saunt was a "being whom vanity had put so off her guard" (93–94).

James insists that his "story must be told by a 3rd person, as it were, a spectator, an observer" who "knows her [Flora Saunt's] case" (Edel and Powers 126). Despite the third-person perspective, the narrator of "Glasses" is initially taken in by Saunt's conceit. Playing the role of subject, Saunt provides an "exquisite figure" for the gaze (and the brush) of James's narrator, a portrait painter. He describes his vision of Flora in the opera box: "Dressed in white, with diamonds in her hair and pearls on her neck, she [Flora Saunt] had a pale radiance of beauty which even at that distance made her a distinguished presence and, with the air that easily attaches to lonely loveliness in public places, an agreeable mystery" (167). Saunt returns the gaze of her admirer: "She presently moved her eyes over the house, and I felt them brush me again like the wings of a dove," the narrator explains. "I don't know what quick pleasure flickered into the hope that she would at last see me. She did see me: she suddenly bent forward to take up the little double-barrelled ivory glass that rested on the edge of the box, and, to all appearance, fix me [*sic*] with it" (169–70). When she lifts her opera glasses, however, she participates in a deception. The validity of her gaze is merely a ruse. Having refused to use consistently corrective spectacles, Saunt has lost her vision.

As the narrator eventually learns, Saunt's enchanting glance is "a vacant, challenging stare" (171). "Playing at perfection" (176), her display in the opera house presents "a perfect imitation" of her former glory—despite the "deep darkness" in which she sits. When the narrator learns of her blindness, he "gasped, but [his] word had come: if she had lost her sight it was in this very loss that she had found again her beauty" (173). In "Glasses," Saunt's husband Geoffrey Dawling, a suitor she originally rejected as "grotesque" (161), enables her vanity rather than reveals it. As he explains to the narrator, "I would take her with leather blinders, like a shying mare!" (131). Ironically, James's narrator gathers comfort "from seeing that if our companion's beauty lived again her vanity partook of its life" (175). For him, the spectacle of display in the opera box immortalizes idealized beauty, making the deception worthwhile.

Pivotal scenes in four of Edith Wharton's works—*The Age of Innocence*, *Old New York*, *The House of Mirth*, and *The Custom of the Country*—also occur in the opera box. In these scenes, Wharton records the conventions of New York's inner circle and traces the transformations wrought by the "Invaders," reflecting on the implications of both. Although, by her own admission, Edith Newbold Jones Wharton's ancestry was "purely middle-class," her family belonged to the same elite group as the "little aristocratic nucleus" of New York society (*A Backward Glance* 11). The lives of these elite were ordered by "upholding two standards of importance in any community, that of education and good manners, and of scrupulous probity in business and private affairs" (21).

In "A Little Girl's New York," published in *Harper's Magazine* several months after Wharton's death, Wharton recorded aspects of the old New York of her childhood that she had omitted in *A Backward Glance*. Reflecting on her past, she discovered that "everything that used to form the fabric of our daily life has been torn in shreds, trampled on, destroyed; and hundreds of little incidents, habits, traditions which, when I began to record my past, seemed too insignificant to set down, have acquired the historical importance of fragments of dress and furniture dug up in a Babylonian tomb" (*Uncollected Critical Writings* 287). Several of these "incidents" are related to her initial experiences with opera. As a young girl of ten, Wharton returned to New York with her family after an extended stay in Europe, and she recalled that "the kindly whiskered gentlemen encouraged her to join in the mild talk" during the traditional after-dinner visits. She remembers that "the conversation ranged safely from Langdons, Van Rensselaers, and Lydigs to Riveses, Duers, and Schermerhorns, with an occasional allusion to the Opera (which there was some talk of transplanting from the old Academy of Music to a 'real' opera House, like Covent Garden or the Scala) [. . .]" (283). Talk of New York's most venerable families and of opera mixed easily in these inner circles of privilege, evidence of their breeding and their customs. As Wharton explains, "in the way of spectacles New York did not as yet provide much. There was in fact only the old Academy of Music, where Campanini, in his prime, warbled to an audience still innocently following the eighteenth-century tradition that the Opera was a social occasion, invented to stimulate conversation [. . .]" (286). When Wharton was considered old enough to attend the operas, the Metropolitan Opera House "was inaugurated, and with it came Wagner, and with Wagner a cultivated and highly musical German audience in the stalls, which made short work of the chatter in the boxes. I well remember the astonishment with which we learned that it was 'bad form' to talk during the acts, and the almost immediate compliance of the box-audience with this new rule of politeness, which thereafter was broken only by two or three thick-skinned new-comers in the social world," Wharton recalls (286).

Although Wharton's life and fiction spanned the turn of the century, *The Age of Innocence* is set in the New York of the 1870s, a decade still ruled by the customs of the old order but already anticipating the changes on the horizon. "On a January evening of the early seventies," Wharton's narrator relates, "Christine Nilsson was singing in *Faust* at the Academy of Music in New York" (3). With these words, Wharton thrusts the reader of *The Age of Innocence* into the socially exclusive world of New York society. In this carefully codified and elitist realm, opera marks the opening of the winter season, "defines those who were members of the inner circle" (Montgomery 22), and exemplifies the wealth and leisure of this class. Serving as a pivotal opening, punctuating the action throughout the novel, and appearing again at the conclusion, opera functions as a structural frame for the work. As Herbert Lindenberger argues in *Opera: The Extravagant Art,* the "operatic and real-life worlds" are both "thoroughly implicated in artifice" (174). By framing several key scenes at the opera, Wharton illustrates the duality of this artifice of performance. Opera, with its "penchant for ceremony and display" (Lindenberger 38), provides the audience an opportunity to gaze upon the embodied exhibition of artistic imagination and passion. Within the opera boxes, where the conventions of "taste" and "form" prevail, members of New York's society participate in their own spectacle of behavior. Both opera and the code of "manners and customs" (Wharton 136) exist within constrained and ordered systems. The artifice of opera allows its participants to express their imagination and passion; however, the artifice of the conventional behavior of the elite stifles its conformists.

In the opening paragraph of the novel, Wharton artfully reveals several key details about the values of New York society. By the end of the 1870s, the upper class would be bitterly divided by controversy over the building of the Metropolitan Opera. As the narrator explains, "Though there was already talk of the erection, in remote metropolitan distances 'above the forties,' of a new Opera House [. . .] the world of fashion was still content to reassemble every winter in the shabby red and gold boxes of the sociable old Academy" (3). While the narrator provides three potential reasons for preserving the tradition of the old Academy, the view attributed to the "conservatives" represents the predominant view of those in authoritative positions. "Conservatives cherished it for being small and inconvenient, and thus keeping out the 'new people' whom New York was beginning to dread and yet be drawn to" (3). John Dizikes explains in *Opera in America: A Cultural History* that, "Musically, [New York] barely supported one opera house. Socially, it needed two" (216).

The old guard of New York's elite, however, did not agree that limited access to the Academy necessitated the building of a new opera house. The Academy of Music, "venerable by New York standards, [was] a symbol of cultural refinement and social standing. The Academy was the hub of the social season and opera boxes were the center of the hub" (Dizikes 216). Because the Academy had only thirty of them, "the boxes rarely changed hands, and then only within a very limited social circle" (Wharton 216). The limited availability of box seats, coupled with a great demand for them, allowed the possessors of opera boxes an enviable position of privilege and prestige. Eventually, the members of old New York society could no longer prevent the "powerful new group of corporate financiers and industrial entrepreneurs, including men such as J. P. Morgan" (Montgomery 23) from building the Metropolitan Opera House. The Met contained "four tiers of boxes" (providing 122 boxes) which would seat 750 persons (Dizikes 218). While the members of New York's society attempted to retain its class interests, the successful newcomers proved that money alone was "thought a rightful basis on which to claim privilege" (Dizikes 218). Newland Archer's New York circle looked on with dismay as men like Julius Beaufort, with a "regrettable past," found success in the business world and gained access to society. Despite the apparent acceptance of Beaufort by the elite, however, its members still persisted in asking themselves behind closed doors, "Who *was* Beaufort?" (Wharton 15).

The elite members of New York society in the 1870s divided the year into two seasons: winter and summer. While the summer months were devoted to travel (either to summer resorts or abroad), "the winter season was marked by the opening of the opera season" (Montgomery 19). By ordering their calendars around events like the opera, these socialites attempted to "establish parity with European metropolitan elites" (Montgomery 22). In addition to serving as a way for the "possessors of great fortunes" to "push themselves forward and claim the social rewards their money entitled them to" (Dizikes 216), opera also allowed them to display publicly the evidences of this status. The society pages of newspapers participated in this spectacle of wealth. Even the "journalists' reports so concentrated on the details of the audience that they sometimes failed to even mention the name of the opera being performed" (Montgomery 135). By situating her characters in an opera box at the Academy during the winter opera season, Wharton underscores the influence of the social and cultural world of spectacle and performance.

As readers, our first introduction to the two main female characters occurs through the lenses of two gentlemen, Newland Archer and Lawrence Lefferts. Like the men gathered in the opera box, we, too, participate in the objectifying gaze. Using the language of performance, Maureen Montgomery explains that the opera productions at the Academy provided a "social space in which gender and class relations were enacted and performed" (18). This theatrical venue served not only as the stage for the musical and dramatic performance by the opera stars but also as the platform for a complex performance of class and gender relations. The spectacle of the women's opera boxes provided an opportunity to demonstrate the wealth and leisure of New York's upper class. Displayed in their evening dresses and jewels, the women embodied the wealth, refinery, and gentility of their stock. The narrator emphasizes May's gentility and refinement as he describes the "warm pink blush" that "suffused the young slope of her breast to the line where it met a modest tulle tucker fastened with a single gardenia" (Wharton 5). In contrast, the reader discovers that Ellen Olenska's "unusual dress" manages to attract a great deal of unsolicited attention because of the "cut of the dark blue velvet gown rather theatrically caught up under her bosom by a girdle with a large old-fashioned clasp" (8). The members of the elite prefer the modesty of May's attire to Ellen's theatricality. While social conventions prevented women from engaging in public affairs, "the rules of the private drawing room prevailed in the opera box and public ballroom, thereby privatizing public space and making it a respectable place for women of the social elite to be seen" (Montgomery 67). Ellen Olenska remains outside this inner circle, however. As Newland observes, "to receive Countess Olenska in the family circle was a different thing from producing her in public, at the Opera of all places" (Wharton 10). Only those women who occupied a clearly defined role within the elite's conventional system could afford to participate in the spectacle of display. For women like Ellen Olenska, such an appearance demonstrated poor taste.

Men who attended the opera, "the carefully-brushed, white-waistcoated, buttonhole-flowered gentlemen who succeeded each other in the club box, exchanged friendly greetings" and then "turned their opera-glasses critically on the circle of ladies who were the product of the system" (Wharton 7). The motivations of the male gaze were numerous. Some, like Newland Archer, looked upon the ladies with a "thrill of possessorship" (6), while those like Lawrence Lefferts looked to see who observed the "intricate and fascinating" details of good "form" (7). The display of women served another practical purpose for these privileged patrons. Customarily, young debutantes, like May Welland, "attend[ed] the opera before going on to private balls. The opera was thereby incorporated into the rituals of the marriage market and the processes that reproduced class" (Montgomery 31). As it was for Newland Archer and May Welland, "the opera house was a marriage market, where young men and women met under the eyes of their elders" (Dizikes 286). Seated between her mother and aunt, May Welland, Newland's "betrothed," presents herself to New York society. As the act on stage comes to an end, Newland feels the "desire to be the first man to enter Mrs. Mingott's box, to proclaim to the waiting world his engagement to May Welland" (Wharton 13). Despite this temporary break with form, Newland's actions clearly communicate his allegiance to and association with the family of his betrothed to the other observers in the boxes. Even though the men openly engaged in the act of gazing upon the women in the opera boxes, the women were forced to feign complete absorption in the performance on stage. The narrator observes May's "absorbed young face" (6), with "eyes ecstatically fixed on the stage-lovers" (5). Likewise, even in the midst of the turmoil her appearance creates, Ellen Olenska "sat gracefully in her corner of the box, her eyes fixed on the stage" (12). After all, these "conventions on which life was molded" (5) were ruled by the "dictates of taste" (12).

Despite the box patrons' apparent lack of attention to the actual opera, the primary performance on stage plays a pivotal role in the novel's development. Although many critics of *The Age of Innocence* have attempted to draw parallels between the story of *Faust* and Wharton's novel, they have overlooked the performance history of the opera in the historical context of Newland's New York world. Gounod's *Faust,* the "staple of New York seasons," opened at the New York Academy of Music on November 25, 1863. Conducted by Max Maretzek, the opera was indeed performed in Italian (just as Newland reports), although the libretto was originally composed in French. Newland Archer attributes this development to "an unalterable and unquestioned law of the musical world" that "required the German text of French operas sung by Swedish artists" to be "translated into Italian for the clearer understanding of English-speaking audiences" (Wharton 4). Rather than a law of the musical world, this adaptation is more accurately attributed to a popular convention of performance in a venue traditionally dominated by Italian operas. Although Clara Louise Kellogg sang the role of Marguerite in *Faust's* debut at the Academy, Christine Nilsson, who had established herself as a great diva in Europe in the 1860s, sang the part at the Academy in New York in the 1870s, and *Faust* "became the most popular opera in America for the next half century" (Dizikes 175, 215).

As Newland Archer enters the opera, Miss Nilsson is singing "*Ill se fait tard,*" or " 'Tis growing late," a duet between Faust and Marguerite at the conclusion of Act 3. Newland, always conscious of convention, knows that it is " 'not the thing' to arrive early at the opera" (Wharton 4). Instead, he arrives at the climax of the performance. In the duet, Marguerite sings a declaration of love to Faust that concludes with these words: "He loves me! My heart is so full! The bird is singing, The winds are sighing! Every voice known in Nature joins the tender refrain: "He loves thee!" (Gounod 175–77). While May Welland's eyes are "ecstatically fixed on the stage-lovers" (Wharton 5) during this tender duet, Newland "turn[s] his eyes from the stage and scan[s] the opposite side of the house" in order to view his intended (5). Thinking about what he presumes to be May's inability to absorb the deeper complexities of the plot, he anticipates his own honeymoon and eventual wooing of May: "We'll read *Faust* together [. . .] by the Italian lakes" (6). Although May's innocence attracts Newland, he imagines himself shattering that innocence on their honeymoon and throughout their marriage. As this scene demonstrates, there are two performances simultaneously occurring at the opera—the actual stage performance and the carefully orchestrated code of conduct in the boxes.

As an opera that "marked the end of the second period of American operatic history and opened the next" (Dizikes 175), *Faust's* position parallels Newland's. Both the opera and the man are standing between two cultural traditions. As Dizikes explains, *Faust* "was the first challenge to the popular supremacy of Verdi and, even more, the first of what would be a number of challenges to the supremacy of all Italian opera. In the next period the language of opera would be French and German" (175). Likewise, the course of Newland Archer's life depends upon the powerful forces of social convention. While he longs to pursue his heart's desires, he chooses instead to conform to the will of an "old-fashioned" artifice (269). Newland remains unable to see that those laws he thought were so "unalterable and unquestioned" (4)—both in opera and in societal codes of conduct—would be unraveled by the next generation. Because he fears the consequences of ignoring society's conventions, he is unwilling to question their usefulness or confront the impact of these laws upon his happiness. As a result, he misses the "flower of life" (258).

The artifice and convention of opera, however, do not prevent the expression of emotion and passion. Indeed, within the confines of predictability (the same score, the same plot, the same outcome), the opera singers manage to wrench a great deal of imagination and passion. The artifice of the form collaborates with the creativity of the artist, thus transforming convention into originality. Newland's inability to merge these two realms—convention and imagination—forces him to choose between them in the "real" world of his life. To compensate for this deficiency, Newland lives between two worlds: the realm of his aesthetic interests—books, art, and opera—and his conventional life as a lawyer, a husband, and a member of New York's elite inner circle. His attempts to keep these two worlds separate often fail. When this failure occurs, he seems unable to distinguish between the "real" world where he lives and the "ideal" world of his own desires. As shown by his conversations with Ellen Olenska, Newland Archer longs to escape these necessary distinctions.

Ellen, who stands outside of the accepted circle of society, understands the protections that social conventions provide—even for herself and for Newland. During the carriage ride from the train station to Granny Mingott's home, Ellen resists Newland's romantic overtures and refuses to join him in his dreams of an ideal world where they can be together. As she explains to him, "we'll look not at visions, but at realities" (Wharton 215). In his passion, Newland denies this assertion of the "real" world. He responds, "I don't know what you mean by realities. The only reality to me is this" (216). Exhibiting his passion and idealism, Newland voices the deepest desires of his heart: "I want—I want somehow to get away with you into a world where words like that [mistress] don't exist" (216). Forcing him to return to the "real" world, Ellen explains to him that there is no such place, and those who have attempted to find it discover that "it wasn't at all different from the old world they'd left, but only rather smaller and dingier and more promiscuous" (216). As Ellen's words reveal, to discover that world would tear the shreds of decency and shatter the fragile code of customs. Recognizing that she, too, remains entrapped by the bonds of social convention, Ellen understands that the protection society provides must not be relinquished. That code of behavior prevents her from becoming a mistress and Newland from spiraling into professional and personal ruin. In a moment of bravery, Newland claims that he is "beyond" caring what the "people who trust them" think (217). Ellen reminds him, however, that he has "never been beyond. And *I* have [. . .] and I know what it looks like there" (217).

Unable to actually wrench himself free from the bonds of convention, Newland retreats to the aesthetic pleasures of books, art, and opera to experience passion and imagination. "Newland Archer prided himself on his knowledge of Italian art. His boyhood had been saturated with Ruskin, and he had read all of the latest books [. . .] and a wonderful new volume called 'The Renaissance' by Walter Pater. He talked easily of Botticelli, and spoke of Fra Angelico with a faint condescension" (Wharton 52). For the most part, however, Newland's uses of these plastic and visual art forms are self-serving. Acting as his own interpreter, he may manipulate his "reading" of these "texts." Wharton frames Newland's use of these art forms as consumptive. As the narrator relates, "He had declined three dinner invitations in favor of this feast; but though he turned the pages with the sensuous joy of the book-lover, he did not know what he was reading, and one book after another dropped from his hand" (104). Feasting and gorging himself on the books, Newland misses the heart of these works of art.

The performatory art forms always elicit an emotional response from Newland and serve as a transforming experience (and not merely a consumptive one). At a performance of *The Shaughraun,* Newland is "moved" by the parting scene. The scene on the stage "made the memory of his last talk with Madame Olenska so vivid to the young man that as the curtain fell on the parting of the two actors his eyes filled with tears, and he stood up to leave the theater" (88). In this performance, the actors on stage embody their characters, and they breathe life into the words of the script, prompting the emotional and imaginative responses of the audience. Similarly, when Newland and May return to see *Faust* with the van der Luydens, the performance on stage prompts Newland to think of Ellen. When Miss Nilsson sings "*M'ama, non m'ama,*" his emotions and memories overwhelm him, prompting him to leave. As art forms that must be experienced, and not just consumed, the performatory arts force the observers to participate. Even as they are engaged in their own spectacle of display, the members of New York's society cannot completely escape the opera's transforming power. Perhaps their penchant for opera comes from a deep desire to participate (even if only vicariously) in the display of passion, emotion, and imagination.

While Newland Archer's gaze introduces the reader to May Welland, the opera glasses of Lawrence Lefferts present the novel's unintentional prima donna, Ellen Olenska. Like the diva on stage, Ellen Olenska, dressed "rather theatrically" (8), attracts the undivided attention of the audience and upstages the other ladies in the box. Ellen, "the wearer of this unusual dress, who seemed quite unconscious of the attention it was attracting, stood a moment in the center of the box" (8). Like the diva on stage, the Countess Olenska embodies the passion, freedom, and imagination that remain suppressed in the conventions of the upper classes. For Ellen, "poetry and art are the breath of life" (119). Her entrance onto the stage of New York society prompts quite a stir. These society patrons do not approve of this diva's appearance on their stage. The authority on taste and form, Lefferts, responds to her arrival with an exclamation: "My God!" (7). Mr. Sillerton Jackson, the expert on "family," remarks, "I didn't think the Mingotts would have tried it on" (9). In their world of "faint implications and pale delicacies" (13), the countess's arrival prompts a whirlwind of speculation and judgment. Ellen feels the intensity of New York's gaze.

She explains to Newland that the arbiters of custom and tradition make her feel as if she is "on stage, before a dreadfully polite audience that never applauds" (100). Ellen recognizes that she never fully gains the approval of society's inner circle, but, like the diva, she accepts symbols of their admiration: flowers. Newland, observing something "rich," "strong," and "full of fiery beauty" in Ellen, sends her a "cluster of yellow roses" which embodies all of those qualities (60). In addition to the roses from Newland, Ellen receives "wonderful orchids" from Beaufort and a "whole hamper of carnations" from Henry van der Luyden (61). Despite these horticultural overtures, the artifice of conventional behavior suffocates her imagination and passion.

One of the few characters who recognizes the artifice surrounding her, Ellen Olenska asserts that New York's code of behavior is a "blind conformity to tradition—somebody else's tradition" (179). With a cosmopolitan spirit, Ellen longs for interaction with "dramatic artists, singers, actors, and musicians" (80). The performative art forms, not simply visual arts, interest Ellen. Like the opera singers, the artists that engage Ellen's attention embody passion, creativity, and imagination. On stage, these performers take the artifice of a drama and breathe life into it. While Newland Archer considers himself "at heart a dilettante" (4), and May believes that he is "artistic" (63), he still clings to the unimaginative traditions of the artifice of social conformity. When Ellen complains that she has "not met a single artist" (79) since her arrival in New York, Newland responds: "What kind of artists? I know one or two painters, very good fellows, that I could bring to see you if you'd allow me" (79). The Countess recognizes, however, that these art forms are merely representations of life on a still frame. She longs for the thrill of the dramatic arts—the embodied arts.

As Beaufort's reply to this exchange between Ellen and Newland suggests, art for the elite merely performs a dutiful function: it demonstrates wealth. Because Beaufort doesn't own any paintings by New York artists, he can't even imagine that they exist. For Beaufort, and even for Newland, the arts serve primarily as commodities to be consumed and displayed for their own pleasure. When Newland Archer meets writers, painters, and musicians, he remains unable to imagine their integration into his own world. "These scattered fragments [the artists] had never shown any desire to be amalgamated with the social structure" (76), and Newland's New York prefers this distance between the bohemians and itself. Newland believes that "if his world [is] small, so [is] theirs, and the only way to enlarge either [is] to reach a stage of manners where they would naturally merge" (77). More comfortable with the performance on the "stage of manners," Newland equates any "unusual situation" with the "unfamiliar" vocabulary that belongs only to "fiction and the stage" (82). He fails to recognize the artifice of the society that controls his actions. The narrator reminds the reader of the extent of this artifice: "In reality, they all lived in a kind of hieroglyphic world, where the real thing was never said or done or even thought, but only represented by a set of arbitrary signs" (34).

The rejection of Ellen and her subsequent restoration illustrate a deep divide in the will of New York society over her reception into its ranks. Similarly, Wharton's references to *Faust* and *La Sonnambula* invoke another occasion of divided loyalties in the ranks of privilege. While New York's inner circle slights Ellen Olenska and foils Mrs. Mingott's attempts to introduce her properly, the van der Luydens redeem the situation. Those who initially rejected Ellen learn of this development at a performance of Bellini's opera, *La Sonnambula,* or "The Sleepwalker." The narrator reports, "That evening at the Opera, Mr. Sillerton Jackson was able to state that the envelope [delivered to Mrs. Mingott's door] contained a card inviting the Countess Olenska to the dinner which the van der Luydens were giving the following weekend" (44). Wharton's choice of operas for this scene is not accidental. Her contemporaries would recall the dispute over New York's two opera houses in the early 1880s. As Dizikes explains, "On the night of October 22, 1883, while Etelka Gerster sang Amina in Bellini's *La Sonnambula* at the Academy, Christine Nilsson inaugurated the Metropolitan as Marguerite in Gounod's *Faust*" (219). "Divided in [their] loyalties" to the two rival opera houses, the members of the upper class showed their allegiance to their house of choice with their attendance that night. Wharton understood the power of New York's elite to promote or condemn anyone or any venture by giving or withholding its financial backing and its social approval. Ellen Olenska and, eventually, Newland Archer learn the necessity of society's sanction and the sting of its rejection.

Just like Faust and Marguerite's, Newland and Ellen's love affair forces them to choose between a life of shared affection (which would doom Faust and Marguerite to hell and banish Newland and Ellen from the circles of friends and family) and a life of resignation to the will of God (in Marguerite's case) or the will of society's conventions. Newland, conforming to the will and expectations of his family and friends, marries May Welland. As Book Two opens at their wedding, Newland Archer associates this occasion with the opening night at the opera. " 'How like a first night at the Opera!' he thought, recognizing all the same faces in the same boxes (no, pews), and wondering if, when the Last Trump sounded, Mrs. Selfridge Merry would be there with the same towering ostrich feathers in her bonnet, and Mrs. Beaufort with the same diamond earrings and the same smile—and whether suitable proscenium seats were already prepared for them in another world" (134–35). The same artifice of convention and the display of wealth and status confront him at his wedding, just as they do at the opera. Newland finds the similarities so striking that he temporarily confuses the pews of the church with the opera boxes at the Academy. All the ladies and gentlemen of the various "tribes" of the upper classes gather to gaze upon the spectacle of a wedding, a rite of nineteenth-century New York that "seemed to belong to the dawn of history" (133). As Newland's association suggests, the opera season also ranked as an indelible part of New York's social life. These rituals of performance and display appear to be so permanent and unalterable that Newland imagines "proscenium seats" for these society divas in "another world."

In the "winter of the second year of [Newland's] marriage" (Wharton 191), the beginning of opera season punctuates the passage of time. "By the fifteenth the season was in full blast, Opera and theaters were putting forth their new attractions, dinner engagements were accumulating, and dates for dances being fixed" (191). The opening of the opera prompts Mrs. Archer to focus on the ways that New York society is changing. While this speculation becomes habitual for Mrs. Archer, Newland eventually assumes her suspicions. He, too, is "obliged to admit that if [New York society] had not actually changed it was certainly changing" (191). With each passing year, the "forms" and "tastes" that dictated his world became more obscure. This "marked trend" (191) of transition and transformation troubles the old stalwarts of New York and dominates the conversation at Mrs. Archer's Thanksgiving dinner. As evidence of this trend, Miss Sophy Jackson points to the "extravagance in dress" that she observes on opening night at the opera (192). For these members of the upper class, the opera had always been a place where "domestic rules of decorum were applied to public space" (Montgomery 51). A violation of the "rigorously adhered to" (Dizikes 285) convention of appropriate attire represented a larger usurping of their code. As further evidence of this change in society, the Sunday evenings at Mrs. Struthers, where Bohemian artists performed, were now tolerated as appropriate. As May explains, "Oh, you know, everybody goes to Mrs. Struther's now; and she was invited to Granny's last reception" (Wharton 193). Once again, once a member of New York society supports something, it soon becomes acceptable. Perhaps this explains the great efforts the elite made to keep the newcomers out of the Academy and its inner circle.

Beaufort's ability to transcend these limitations, however, predicts the eventual change in the composition and behavior of New York society. By the end of the novel, when Newland's son Dallas announces his intentions to marry Beaufort's daughter Fanny, the change in the attitudes of the elite is evident. As the narrator explains, "Nobody was narrow-minded enough to rake up against her [Fanny] the half-forgotten facts of her father's past and her own origin" (262). The society that remained "distrustful and afraid" of Ellen Olenska (even as it admired her) took Fanny "joyfully for granted" (262). "Only the older people remembered so obscure an incident in the business life of New York as Beaufort's failure" (262). While Newland relinquishes the object of his affections because he fears the societal repercussions, Dallas takes "for granted that his family [will] approve" of his fiancée (263).

One of the major threats that disturbed the equilibrium of this inner circle of New York was the rumor of Beaufort's financial ruin. Yet, when Mrs. Beaufort appears at the opera, "wearing her old smile and a new emerald necklace" (200), she temporarily appeases those worries. Participating in the greatest spectacle of artifice, Mrs. Beaufort's ruse attempts to pacify the fears of New York society. By parading the symbols of wealth and power—her jewels—and submitting herself for public display, Mrs. Beaufort contrives to create an illusion of permanency and stability. In an earlier scene at the opera, Wharton intentionally associates Mrs. Beaufort with the adornments and trappings of wealth. In the opening pages of the novel, Mrs. Beaufort "as usual appeared in her box just before the Jewel Song" (16). In this aria, Marguerite discovers the casket of jewels that Faust, assisted by Mephistopheles, uses to tempt her. Marguerite sings these words:

> Ah! the joy past compare,
> These jewels bright to wear!
> Is it thou, Marguerite, is it thou?
> Now reply, now reply!
> Tell me, tell me, tell me truly.
> No, no! this is not I!
> No surely enchantment is o'er me!
> Some king's daughter I spy,
> This is not I,
> All are bending before me!
> Ah, might it only be!
> Were he but here to see!
> Now as a royal lady
> He would indeed adore me!
> Ah! For as a royal lady he would now adore me! Here are more, ready to adorn me!
> I can hardly wait to try on this bracelet here, the necklace yon!
> Ah! it is like a hand laid on my arm to oppress me!
> Ah, the joy past compare,
> These jewels bright to wear! (Gounod 127–31)

Marguerite recognizes that the jewels represent an imagined identity of wealth and grandeur. She manages to make a distinction between herself and her bejeweled countenance. Ultimately, however, Faust's ruse works. Captivated by the jewels' charms (and Faust's), the vision orchestrated by Mephistopheles succeeds. Like the spectacle of jewels in *Faust,* Mrs. Beaufort's display is a deceptive device. Her performance, however, depends upon the jewels. Mrs. Beaufort's attempts to sustain this performance are as impotent as the inner circle's efforts to sustain its own elaborate code of artifice. When Regina Beaufort tries to fall back upon her own respectable ancestry by reclaiming her identity as Regina Dallas, Mrs. Mingott reminds her that her name was Beaufort "when he covered you with jewels, and it's got to stay Beaufort now that he's covered you with shame" (203). The jewels that once represented her wealth and power now mark her as tainted by disgrace and rejected by society.

In the aftermath of Beaufort's failure, the van der Luydens come to town because they " 'owed it to society' to show themselves at the Opera" (236) in the face of such turmoil. The economic and social stability of this elite group relies on these artificial performances. The members of the inner circle must believe in the invincibility of its order, custom, and predictability. (This explains New York's willingness to reevaluate Ellen Olenska after the van der Luydens' dinner). Once again, an appearance at the opera is used to bolster the stability of the inner circle. The van der Luydens "invited Sillerton Jackson, Mrs. Archer and Newland and his wife to go with them to the Opera, where *Faust* was being sung for the first time that winter" (236). Indeed, every detail about the scene parallels the first: the same opera, *Faust;* the same diva, Christine Nilsson; and the same song, "*M'ama, non M'ama.*" With this trip to the opera, Wharton returns us to the opening scene of the novel. The irony of this occasion is not lost on Newland Archer. He sat watching the "same scene he had looked at, two years previously, on his first meeting with Ellen Olenska" (238). Rather than remembering that earlier occasion as the night he admired May and announced his engagement, he recollects his first glance of Ellen. As he once again turns his gaze away from the stage and to the opera boxes, he "half-expected [Ellen] to appear again in old Mrs. Mingott's box, but it remained empty" (238). For the van der Luydens and the other members of their party, this return to the opera is a symbol of stability and predictability in their world. For Newland, however, the occasion serves as a painful reminder of all he has lost. An "uncontrollable longing seized him to tell [May] the truth, to throw himself on her generosity, and ask for the freedom he had once refused" (239). For once, the passion embodied on the stage (as Marguerite thrills in the recognition of Faust's love) moves Newland. Overwhelmed by this desire, Newland defies one of the conventions of his world when he enters Mrs. van der Luyden's box during a solo and feigns a headache in order to return home and tell May the truth.

Newland's defiance of convention comes too late. May, whose "niceness" (according to Newland) is a "curtain dropped before an emptiness" (157), successfully enacts the ultimate performance of artifice. Recognizing the threat that Ellen Olenska and all of her passion poses to her marriage, May contrives a clever ruse of deception. She isolates Ellen and secures Newland by announcing her pregnancy, and she closes the ranks of New York's inner circle in her defense. May and the other adherents to convention convince Newland and Ellen that their artifice protects its members from self-destruction. The conclusion of the opera that frames the novel supports May's triumph. The forbidden love affair of Faust and Marguerite damns his soul and imprisons her. Like Ellen Olenska, Marguerite achieves redemption only by repenting of her sins and relinquishing her lover. Unbridled passion and fulfillment are not allowed to triumph—even on the opera stage. The dual performances—the one on the stage and the one in the opera box—converge. Artifice triumphs.

In "New Year's Day," the story marking the 1870s in Wharton's *Old New York*, the opera box provides the setting for another performance of artifice and display. The story is told as the narrator's recollection, and these memories are prompted when his cousin Hubert Wesson invites him to join Mrs. Hazeldean, the young society widow of Charles Hazeldean, at the opera. The narrator relates that "in Mrs. Hazeldean's box I was only an overgrown boy again, bathed in such blushes as used, at the same age, to visit Hubert, forgetting that I had a moustache to twirl, and knocking my hat from the peg on which I had hung it, in my zeal to pick up a programme she had not dropped" (293). The "formidably lovely" (293) lady that the young men accompany at the opera is there alone—a violation of New York's code of conduct. "There was no other lady in Mrs. Hazeldean's box when we entered; none joined her during the evening, and our hostess offered no apology for her isolation," the narrator relates. "In the New York of my youth every one knew what to think of a woman who was seen 'alone at the opera';

if Mrs. Hazeldean was not openly classed with Fanny Ring, our one conspicuous 'professional,' it was because, out of respect for her social origin, New York preferred to avoid such juxtapositions" (295). Mrs. Hazeldean has exhibited an independence from and disregard for the traditions and codes of New York society. When the narrator enters Mrs. Hazeldean's box, his mother's condemning words from so many years ago came back to him: "She was *bad*. . .always. They used to meet at the Fifth Avenue Hotel" (229).[5] While there were many sights to entice a young boy the day of the great fire—fire engines, carriages, frantic people—the one that captured the attention of young and old alike was the brief glimpse of Lizzie Hazeldean and Henry Prest, a dashing young bachelor, fleeing the burning hotel together, a sight that confirmed society's suspicions. Years after the hotel fire, the narrator establishes a friendship with Mrs. Hazeldean and learns her account of the affair.

Charles Hazeldean, suffering from the "Hazeldean heart," died after only nine years of marriage to Lizzie. He had been "brought up in the old New York tradition, which decreed that a man, at whatever cost, must provide his wife with what she had always 'been accustomed to'; and he had gloried too much in her prettiness, her elegance, her easy way of wearing her expensive dresses, and his friends' enjoyment of the good dinners she knew how to order, not to accustom her to everything which could enhance such graces" (272). The young lawyer's extended illness, however, prevented him from maintaining an income sufficient to keep his wife in this "accustomed" style. Unable to deny him this one pleasure, Lizzie Hazeldean keeps up appearances by supplementing her income. By prostituting herself to her lover, Henry Prest, Lizzie acquired the necessary money. At Charles's death, Prest proposes. Lizzie rejects his offer of marriage, confessing that, for her, their relationship was merely a mercenary one. Refusing his proposal, however, she relinquishes the social protection that marriage would have afforded a young widow. After learning about Mrs. Hazeldean's motives for her scandalous actions, the young narrator comments on his own "confused sense of the complexity—or the chaos—of human relations" (298). Through his encounter with Mrs. Hazeldean, he discovers that the web of human interactions is not as easily negotiated as the conventions of his class supposed them to be.

By placing Mrs. Hazeldean in the opera box, Wharton invokes class and gender dynamics. As one of the acceptable venues for public amusement, the opera provided the upper class with an ideal opportunity for intermingling. Strict rules of etiquette guided these interactions, however. Maureen Montgomery explains: "Women were allowed to receive calls in their box under the same rules governing calls at home, but women were not allowed to visit other boxes. At most, they could accompany their male escort on a promenade within the theater, bowing to friends on passing but not allowing other gentlemen to join them, and not stopping to speak with them—just as though they were in a public thoroughfare" (127). Likewise, Florence Hartley's *The Ladies' Book of Etiquette, and Manual of Politeness* instructed young ladies: "Do not accept an invitation to visit any place of public amusement, with a gentleman with whom you are but slightly acquainted, unless there is another lady also invited. You may, as a young lady, go with a relative or your fiancé, without a chaperon, but not otherwise" (172). Lizzie Hazeldean's solitary confinement in the opera box indicates her rejected status.

In addition to sorting out the dynamics of class, the opera box also facilitated a complex dynamic of gender relationships. As the opera scene in *The Age of Innocence* demonstrates, women in the opera boxes submitted themselves for display, but the rules of etiquette prevented the women from returning the gaze of an admirer. Hartley's etiquette manual explains: "Do not look round the house with your glass. A lady's deportment should be very modest in a theatre" (173). Inevitably, then, "the gender dynamics of display and spectatorship in such venues as the opera house is [*sic*] in some ways suggestive of brothel behavior, with men ogling women framed and contained in boxes in darkened auditoriums" (Montgomery 128). Montgomery goes on to explain that "theaters had not entirely rid themselves of associations with prostitution. As already noted, male spectatorship in theaters did undergo a disciplining process, but because it was legitimized within the theater and prosthetically enhanced with the use of binoculars, ogling continued surreptitiously" (128). Wharton explicitly addresses the inadequacies of a social code that sacrifices its women to the self-deprecating acts of prostitution—literally or figuratively. As Lizzie boldly explains to her former lover, Henry Prest, "You thought I was a lovelorn mistress; and I was only an expensive prostitute" (284). Rather than denying the transgression that has alienated her from the inner circle, Lizzie Hazeldean openly confesses it. When she submits herself to the gendered gaze at the opera, she indirectly acknowledges the inevitability of being consumed by those who control the economic market—the male members of society.

Set some thirty years after *The Age of Innocence* and "New Year's Day," Wharton's *The House of Mirth* portrays the transformations of New York society after it embraced Fifth Avenue and its new class of wealth. Like Lizzie Hazeldean, Lily Bart, the heroine of *The House of Mirth,* must rely on the attentions of wealthy men for social and economic security. Although society women's options for acceptable public amusements had expanded since the 1870s, the opera continued to play a key role for those wishing to negotiate and to dominate the circles of privilege. Talking with Lily Bart in Mr. Rosedale's box seat, George Dorset complains about the season's predictability: "Well, here we are, in for another six months of caterwauling. Not for a shade of difference between this year and last, except that the women have got new clothes and the singers haven't got new voices" (94). As Dorset's disparaging comments reveal, he doesn't appreciate the artistry of opera. Instead, he tolerates it as a part of his set's social calendar. He continues by explaining that "my wife's musical, you know—puts me through a course of this every winter. It isn't so bad on Italian nights—then she comes late, and there's time to digest. But when they give Wagner we have to rush dinner, and I pay for it. And the draughts are damnable—asphyxia in front and pleurisy in the back" (94). Although New York's increasingly sophisticated audience demanded an expanded fare of German opera, many society patrons like Dorset continued to exhibit little interest in opera beyond its role in displaying wealth.

In the early pages of *The House of Mirth,* Wharton stages a crucial scene in the opera box. By placing Lily Bart, a young woman "always inspirited by the prospect of showing her beauty in public" (91), in Mr. Rosedale's box on the opening night of the opera season, Wharton puts her heroine in the company of high society and under the surveillance of its gatekeepers. This scene establishes the reputation and identification that make it impossible for Lily to attain a respectable husband and fortune. While showing off her undeniable beauty, the public display in the opera box also confirms Lily's naiveté about the repercussions of her exhibition. The narrator reports that, "conscious tonight of all the added enhancements of her dress, the insistency of Trenor's gaze merged itself in the general stream of admiring looks of which she felt herself the centre." Tonight, Lily thought that "it was good to be young, to be radiant, to glow with the sense of slenderness, strength and elasticity, of well-poised lines and happy tints, to feel one's self lifted to a height apart by that incommunicable grace which is the bodily counterpart of genius!" (91). As a young, unmarried woman, Lily Bart is within the bounds of polite behavior to attend the opera and participate in the spectacle of display. What she doesn't understand is that her display acquires a different meaning—one normally associated with married women. According to Maureen Montgomery, married women's public display "was intended to provoke in other men the envy of the women's 'possessor'—the man who paid for her clothes and jewelery [*sic*]" (128).

The narrator reveals Lily's misstep: "If Lily's poetic enjoyment of the moment was undisturbed by the base thought that her gown and opera cloak had been indirectly paid for by Gus Trenor, the latter had not sufficient poetry in his composition to lose sight of these prosaic facts" (91). In the codified realm of fashionable society, Lily's circumstances suggest that she is Trenor's lover. While he feasts upon her with his eyes, he grows envious that he hasn't actually received any "payment" on his investment: "He knew only that he had never seen Lily look smarter in her life, that there wasn't a woman in the house who showed off good clothes as she did, and that hitherto he, to whom she owed the opportunity of making this display, had reaped no return beyond that of gazing at her in company with several hundred other pairs of eyes" (91). Wrapped up in the splendid illusion of the evening's glamour, Lily is surprised to find herself alone with Trenor between acts. "Trenor said, without preamble, and in a tone of sulky authority: 'Look here, Lily, how is a fellow ever to see anything of you? I'm in town three or four days a week, and you know a line to the club will always find me, but you don't seem to remember my existence nowadays unless you want to get a tip out of me" (91–92). Lily has failed to recognize that by using Trenor for financial assistance, she has compromised her reputation.

Wharton recognized the theatricality of New York society. As the scene at the opera house demonstrates, the customs originally cultivated by the leisure class have been usurped by a new class of society climbers. Lawrence Selden explains the matter to Lily Bart. "The queer thing about society is that the people who regard it as an end are those who are in it, and not the critics on the fence. It's just the other way with most shows—the audience may be under the illusion, but the actors know that real life is on the other side of the footlights. The people who take society as an escape from work are putting it to its proper use; but when it becomes the thing worked for it distorts all the relations of life" (56). Lily Bart, an orphan without the protection of family or fortune, is deluded into thinking that by her own efforts she can ascend the ranks of the influential elite. Tragically, she learns that "life on the other side of the footlights" is brutal and unforgiving.

In *The Custom of the Country*, Wharton's tragedy of manners, New York's Dutch-descended aristocrats and the Wall Street/Fifth Avenue set (the "Invaders") collide. Undine Spragg, a young woman who moves to New York from the Midwestern town of Apex in the hopes of garnering a well-to-do husband, gathers her information about fashionable people, manners, and amusements from the pages of society columns in magazines like *Town Talk* and the *Radiator*. "Fiercely independent" and yet "passionately imitative" (19), Undine lacks an intimate connection in the complex social world she longs to infiltrate; her father's fortune is her only calling card. In striking contrast, Undine's first romantic interest in New York, Ralph Marvell, enters the world of privilege by birth.

> Nothing in the Dagonet and Marvell tradition was opposed to this desultory dabbling with life. For four or five generations it had been the rule of both houses that a young fellow should go to Columbia or Harvard, read law, and then lapse into more or less cultivated inaction. The only essential was that he should live "like a gentleman"—that is, with a tranquil disdain for

> mere money-getting, a passive openness to the finer sensations, one or two fixed principles as to the quality of wine, and an archaic probity that had not yet learned to distinguish between private and "business" honour. (75)

In Undine's relentless and selfish pursuit of life among the fashionable set, the two scenes at the opera offer the only occasions when she registers the sting of rejection and recognizes her exemption from the inner circle.

Chapter 4 opens with Undine's plea: "Father, you've got to take a box for me at the opera next Friday. [. . .] Friday's the stylish night, and that new tenor's going to sing again in 'Cavaleeria' " (41). She makes her request without knowing how much a box costs, and she fails to pronounce the opera correctly or to recall the tenor's name. The importance of the opera for Undine is strictly social. A practical man, Mr. Spragg inquires, "Wouldn't a couple of good orchestra seats do you?" (41). Unlike his daughter, he knows that "a parterre box costs a hundred and twenty-five dollars a night" (43), making it—he implies—a very frivolous indulgence. The father panders to her whims, however, taking an opera box for the season. Enthroned in her box seat, Undine relishes the opportunity to exercise the "gesture[s] learned during her apprenticeship in the stalls" (60), an apprenticeship of observation and imitation. "She had looked down at them, enviously, from the balcony—she had looked up at them, reverentially, from the stalls," the narrator relates, "but now at last she was on a line with them, among them, she was part of the sacred semicircle whose privilege it is, between the sets, to make the mere public forget that the curtain has fallen" (60). As Dizikes explains, the Metropolitan Opera House of 1883 was a "semi-circle of boxes with an opera house built around them, a private club to which the general public was somewhat grudgingly admitted" (218). Ironically, "by the standards of the late nineteenth century, the proportion of boxes was extraordinary" (218), diminishing its marked exclusivity. With 122 boxes, seating 750 people, the Metropolitan offered the prestige of box seating to those who would afford to purchase one. Dizikes describes their position: "On the ground floor there were twelve huge boxes, derisively known as *bagnoir* (bathing) boxes, because they resembled immense bathtubs. Above these was the first tier of thirty-eight boxes, the most prized location in the house, reserved exclusively for stockholders. The next tier had thirty-six boxes, also reserved for stockholders. Above this was a fourth tier of thirty-six boxes, most of which were available for yearly rent by nonstockholders" (218). Although initially thrilled with the sensation of possessing a parterre box opposite the Van Degens, Undine gradually "blushes with anger at her own simplicity in fancying that he [Ralph Marvell] had been 'taken' by her—that she could ever really count among these happy self-absorbed people! They had all their friends, their ties, their delightful crowding obligations: why should they make room for an intruder in a circle so packed with the initiated?" (62).

Undine and her guest, Mabel Lipscomb, are clearly unfamiliar with the rules of etiquette governing a lady's behavior at the opera. Florence Hartley's etiquette book commanded young women to "not look round the opera house with your glass" and to "avoid carefully every motion or gesture that will attract attention." Hartley explains that "to flirt a fan, converse in whispers, indulge in extravagant gestures of merriment or admiration, laugh loudly or clap your hands together, are all excessively vulgar and unlady-like. Never turn your head to look at those seated behind you, or near you" (173–74). Between the two of them, Undine and Mabel violate all of these instructions. When the curtain falls after the first act, "Undine, for the moment unconscious of herself, swe[eps] the house with her opera-glass, searching for familiar faces" (61). Mabel Lipscomb, also searching the crowd, makes "large signs across the house with fan and play-bill" (63). After Mabel spies Marvell in the audience, she alerts Undine with "another conspicuous outbreak of signaling" (64) by "beckoning" (65) him to their box, even though "no one else was wagging and waving in that way: a gestureless mute telegraphy seemed to pass between the other boxes" (63). Mabel doesn't realize that rules of etiquette instruct that "if at the theater, opera, or in a concert-room, you see an acquaintance, you are not expected to recognize her, unless near enough to speak. A lady must not bow to any one, even her own sister, across a theatre or concert-room" (Hartley 177). As the evening wore on, "the leaden sense of failure overcame [Undine] again. Here was the evening nearly over, and what had it led to? Looking up from the stalls, she had fancied that to sit in a box was to be in society—now she saw it might but emphasize one's exclusion. And she was burdened with the box for the rest of the season!" (68). Although the evening at the opera does not end in total failure—Marvell eventually enters Undine's box for a social call—the experience temporarily humbles the young Apex debutante and makes clear her status as an "Invader."

The second scene at the opera occurs many years later, after Undine's divorce from Marvell. Although Undine achieves her initial goal of marrying into New York's upper crust, she quickly becomes discontented.

> She had found out that she had given herself to the exclusive and the dowdy when the future belonged to the showy and the promiscuous; that she was in the case of those who have cast in their lot with a fallen cause, or—to use an analogy more within her range—who have hired an opera box on the wrong night. It was all confusing and exasperating. Apex ideals had been based on the myth of "old families" ruling New York from a throne of Revolutionary tradition, with the new millionaires paying them feudal allegiance. But experience had long since proved the delusiveness of the simile. (193)

In her never-ending effort to gain access to the fashionable set, Undine pursues a romance with a married man from the Fifth Avenue set, Peter Van Degen, believing that the affair will eventually result in his desire to marry her. To that end, she divorces her own husband only to discover that Van Degen refuses to relinquish his claim to respectability by divorcing his patrician wife. With her divorce, Undine finds herself ostracized from the old New York families and the fashionable set. When she returns "midseason" to New York as a divorcée, she once again reads the society column, whose "perusal produced the impression that the season must be the gayest New York had ever known" (371). Her discontent prompts her to ask her father to "take her to the opera that evening" (372). Remembering her previous request for access to the opera, Mr. Spragg assumes that she wants him "to go round and hire a box," but Undine "coloured at the infelicitous allusion: besides, she knew now that the smart people who were 'musical' went in stalls" (372).

With this comment, however, Undine once again reveals her ignorance about the culture and custom of New York society. While it was true that an increasingly knowledgeable audience frequented the Metropolitan Opera House and encouraged the reign of German works, that movement did not originate with the upper crust. The wealthy elite still reigned from their boxes. Undine and her father's stalls "were in the middle of the house, and around them swept the great curve of boxes at which Undine had so often looked up in the remote Stentorian [a New York hotel] days. Then all had been one indistinguishable glitter, now the scene was full of familiar details: the house was thronged with people she knew, and every box seemed to contain a parcel of her past" (373). Seated in the stalls, Undine discovers her mistake. She realizes that she and her father are "merely part of the invisible crowd out of range of the exploring opera glasses," and "perceiv[ing] that no one noticed her" she "felt a defiant desire to make herself seen" (373). Rather than exiting the opera through the door they entered, Undine directs her father to the stockholders' entrance, "press[ing] her way among the furred and jeweled ladies waiting for their motors" (373). Instead of finding herself embraced by her old set, however, she is shunned. By attending the opera, Undine subjects herself to humiliation, and "she had never hated her life as she hated it then" (376). The evening at the opera "had shown her the impossibility of remaining in New York. She had neither the skill nor the power to fight the forces of indifference leagued against her: she must get away at once, and try to make a fresh start" (377). For the second time in the novel, the opera house reminds Undine that she does not belong in the inner circle. Indeed, she spends the next several years in Paris, and when she returns to New York it is as the bride of Elmer Moffat, the quintessential Apex "Invader."

For James and Wharton, the opera box provided the ideal setting for dramatizing the forms and tastes of an age in transition. Familiar with the aristocratic code of manners, these two writers placed their characters in a setting ruled simultaneously by etiquette and spectacle. The opera box captured the essence of the former age of conspicuous leisure and the competing trend of conspicuous consumption. Engaging in the display of wealth, women, and privilege, the box occupants participated in a complicated performance.

Coda

Reverberating Voices

For many readers, the "operatic" suggests absurdity, irrationality, and extravagance. Despite the undisputed canonical status of some of the works included in this study, others might be described in similarly operatic (and disparaging) terms: contrived, artificial, or bizarre. Precisely for this reason, opera offers an important yet underutilized critical lens in the works of Walt Whitman, Edgar Allan Poe, Louisa May Alcott, Kate Chopin, Willa Cather, Henry James, and Edith Wharton. These writers recognize that opera's deviations from "normal" modes of expression enable the artist (literary or musical) to communicate with the audience, engaging the topic of subjectivity directly.

The works considered in this study resist easy categorizations. While they may not represent the whole of American literature, they do suggest that opera—the art form and the cultural context—permeated the poetry and fiction of notable male and female authors. As John Dizikes explains in *Opera in America: A Cultural History,* "The explosive energy, the massed choral power, and the soaring individual voices of opera corresponded to the infinitely mixed voices of the American people" (119). From its first performance on American soil, opera left reverberations that continue to echo in our literature and our culture. Although initial reactions to this foreign art form rejected it as an "unnatural bantling" ("The Opera" 239), Whitman extended opera's reach beyond its performance halls, translating its beauty and passion for humanity. Alcott, Chopin, and Cather discovered in the diva a model of female artistic expression. Poe, James, and Wharton recognized in opera performance a medium for illustrating the carefully codified realm of wealth and leisure. Reading these works through the lens of the opera glass revitalizes canonical classics with a cultural relevance these artists certainly intended, and it enriches our appreciation of works that might otherwise remain in relative obscurity.

Whitman would not be surprised to learn that Americans have

adopted the art form and made it their own. Contemporary novelists continue to invoke opera as a way of making us ask important questions about the role of the artist and the role of the audience. Great American literary classics have been adapted into operatic form: *The Fall of the House of Usher* (Philip Glass), *Little Women* (Mark Adamo), *Washington Square* (Thomas Pasatieri), *The Wings of the Dove* (Douglas Moore), *An American Tragedy* (Tobias Picker), *The Great Gatsby* (John Harbison), *The Crucible* (Robert Ward), *A View from the Bridge* (William Bolcom), *Of Mice and Men* (Carlisle Floyd), and *A Streetcar Named Desire* (André Previn). While not exhaustive, this list illustrates the scope and diversity of American literature in the canon of opera. The connection between American literature and opera invites and requires our critical attention. After listening to the operatic voices in these works, we join Whitman in saying, "Never more shall I escape, never more the reverberations, / [. . .] be absent from me" ("Out of the Cradle," lines 152–53).

Notes

INTRODUCTION

1. For a complete account of the various opera performances and concerts by operatic stars given at these theaters, see Chapter 1 of Krehbiel's *Chapters of Opera.*

2. While many small theaters in nineteenth-century America were referred to as opera houses, many were merely venues for other kinds of theatrical performances. All of the opera houses mentioned in this introduction, however, were built primarily for operatic performances, although most of them hosted other kinds of performances, too.

3. After its desertion in the summer of 1847, Palmo's Opera House became Burton's Theater in 1848. In 1851, the Astor Place Opera House was sold and converted into a library.

4. For a more extensive discussion of the founding of the Metropolitan Opera House, see "The Building of the Metropolitan Opera House," in John Dizikes's *Opera in America* or pages 134–35 in Allen Churchill's *The Upper Crust: An Informal History of New York's Highest Society.*

5. Ironically, the *Casta diva* aria is sung by Norma in Bellini's *Norma,* the same opera that Alcott includes in "The Rival Prima Donnas."

6. *Undoing* is Catherine Clément's term from her book *Opera, or the Undoing of Women* (1979).

CHAPTER 1

1. In her essay "Walt Whitman and Music," Louise Pound notes that while Whitman was in New Orleans, opera was presented four times a week.

2. Many scholars who have explored the significance of opera in Whitman's work, like Wayne Koestenbaum, appropriate Whitman for lesbian and gay studies, focusing on the sexual stimuli that prompt bodily responses in his poetry. These critics argue that Whitman's poetry, like opera, subverts gender norms and creates an inhabitable space for the affinities of "closeted" desires. Quoting excerpts from *Leaves of Grass,* Koestenbaum argues that Whitman's allusions to opera are "queer moments." Similarly, Lawrence Kramer claims that "Whitman's operatic sexuality allows him to float or surge from one position to the other, to become his own circulation between the 'homosexual' bliss of penetration and the 'heterosexual' bliss of abjection" (*After the Lovedeath* 150–51). These critics assert that Whitman's "liquid world" (*New York Dissected* 22) is an "aesthetic-libidinal column or stream that pulses from the orb by which one body is opened and glides into the orifices that rescue another body from being closed" (Kramer 151). Whitman, however, affirms the substantive reality and the metaphysical reality of his responses to opera; he is the "poet of the Body" and the "poet of the Soul" ("Song of Myself," line 422).

3. A notable opera and literature critic, Lawrence Kramer, considers the operatic link between life and death in Whitman's poetry. According to Kramer, Whitman admires Italian opera because of the " 'the electric, pensive, turbulent, artificial' theater of sexual violence" (*After the Lovedeath* 55). Claiming that Whitman's "love for this particular art bespeaks a taste for eroticized suffering," Kramer believes that opera allows Whitman to "become both the dagger and the body that sheathes it" (57). As Kramer accurately observes, all of the operas that Whitman includes in "Proud Music of the Storm" are "caught up in the same sexual economy of (dis)possession (in)fidelity, and violence" (57).

Rather than understanding the sexual violence of opera as the "undoing of women" (Catherine Clément's term), Whitman celebrates the "gender synergy" (Kramer 55) of opera's desire and violence. Kramer's criticism possesses its own agenda, however. Like many others, he focuses on Whitman's own sexuality as a lens for reading the poetry, looking for ways to trace the polarity of male and female, homosexual and heterosexual. While Whitman unquestionably celebrates the human body and sexuality—both male and female—in his poetry, his mode of entry into these erotic zones is a combination of vision and voice. Rather than beginning with the body's sexual reaction, he observes the sights and listens to the sounds around him, translating these into the consuming passions of the body. Opera provides a model for and language for describing not only the passion of human sexuality but also the link between life, death, and immortality. As a spectator at the opera, Whitman not only observes the bodies and movements of the singers, but he also hears the rapturous sounds of their voices.

CHAPTER 2

1. Most of the theatres or "opera houses" that hosted operatic performances also offered other theatrical amusements. So, the narrator clarifies that the bill for that evening is opera.

2. For a more complete consideration of the role of vision and perception in Poe's other tales, see the following sources: "'If This I Saw': The Optic Dilemmas in Poe's Writings" by Judith Saunders; "The Distorted Perception of Poe's Comic Narrators" by James W. Gargano; "Edgar Allan Poe: The Sublime and the Grotesque" by Frederick L. Burwick; and *The Rationale of Deception in Poe* by David Ketterer.

3. David Ketterer uses this term to describe Poe's use of perception in his tales. As he explains, "When man learns to view reality as a continuum, the lines that separate one thing from another blur and dissolve to reveal the shifting and fluid state, the quicksand, which may allow a perception of ideal reality. The arabesque designs are active symbols of Poe's efforts to melt away the rigid pattern that is imposed by man's reason" (36).

4. Believing that the melodramatic ending of "The Rival Prima Donnas" would be suitable for the stage, Alcott converted the work into a play. Assisted by her uncle, Dr. Charles Windship, she submitted the script to Thomas Barry, the manager of the Boston Theatre, "the great theatre on Washington Street, the largest and most elegant in the country" (Stern 188). Although assured that her work would grace the stage, it was never performed. Ironically, on the same night that she met with Thomas Barry about the pro-

duction's prospects, Alcott attended a performance of Bellini's *Norma,* the same opera she alludes to in her short story, at the Boston Theatre. In a letter addressed to Anna Alcott, dated November 6, 1856, Alcott credits that occasion as the "first time in my life I understood how one could go crazy over Operas" (Myerson, Shealy, and Stern 24).

5. "Feminine Endings" is Susan McClary's term and the title of her 1991 study *Feminine Endings: Music, Gender, and Sexuality.*

CHAPTER 3

1. In his editorial notes to the *Prelude and Transfiguration from Tristan and Isolde,* Robert Bailey notes that "the person responsible for this misleading change seems to have been none other than Franz Liszt, who in 1867 made a piano transcription of Isolde's monologue [. . .] and called it Isolden's *Liebes-Tod*" (42).

2. In 1968, Richard Giannone's groundbreaking study, *Music in Willa Cather's Fiction,* recognized the value of music as "a way into [understanding] the evolution of [Cather's] art" (13), opening up new horizons of interpretation for Cather scholars. As Merrill M. Skaggs notes in "Key Modulations in Cather's Novels about Music," Giannone "showed the way for many excellent textual studies to follow by demonstrating the subtlety, density, allusiveness, and coherence of Cather's work as a whole" (25).

3. *Tannhäuser* premiered at the Dresden Opera, *Hofoper,* on October 19, 1845. Not only does Thea Kronborg debut in the role of Elizabeth, but she makes the debut in the opera house where Wagner's work was first performed.

4. As Janis Stout notes in the introduction to her *Calendar of Letters,* "When Willa Cather died on April 24, 1947, her Last Will and Testament included a provision that has severely hampered the study of her work: a prohibition on publishing her letters, either in whole or in part" (xi). When Congress passed the Copyright Extension Act in 1998, the term of protection for unpublished material was extended to seventy years beyond death, so "Cather's letters will not become public domain until 2017" (xi). As a result, I am relying on Stout's paraphrase of this letter.

CHAPTER 4

1. Wharton's derisive term from *The Custom of the Country* for the new wealth that infiltrated New York's inner circle of privilege.

2. For an overview of the various uses of opera in James's fiction, refer to Chapter 12, "Wallowing in a Libretto: James and the Opera," in Adeline Tintner's *The Cosmopolitan World of Henry James.* In "Romance and the Prima Donna Image in the Fiction of Henry James," Peter J. Dyson considers the role of the prima donna and the nature of romance in James's *The Portrait of a Lady,* "The Two Faces," and "The Velvet Glove." Gary Lemco's "Henry James and Richard Wagner: *The American*" argues that James's *The American* has "correspondences in the myth of *Lohengrin,* and possibly in the Medieval Romance of *Tristan and Iseult*" (47). Other scholars, like Laura F. Hodges, have noted the importance of music in James's fiction. Hodges's "Recognizing 'False Notes': Musical Rhetoric in *The*

Portrait of a Lady" claims that "musical referents constitute a 'rhetoric' that James uses to direct our understanding of Isabel's plight and developing consciousness" (2). Some other recent criticism, like *Opera and the Novel: The Case of Henry James* by Michael Halliwell, explores the adaptation of James's fiction into operas.

3. In *The American Scene*, James compares a "charming country-house" in the New England countryside to an opera box. The analogy demonstrates his focus on analyzing the manners and customs of the inhabitants. He explains, "Here, at least, where a small and charming country-house had seated itself very much as the best box, on the most expensive tier, rakes the prospect for grand opera—here might manners too be happily studied, save perhaps for their being enjoyed at too short range" (22).

4. In "Poe's 'The Spectacles' and James's 'Glasses,'" a note published in *Poe Studies* 9 (June 1976), and later reprinted in *The Book World of Henry James: Appropriating the Classics*, Adeline Tintner suggests that the connection between Edgar Allan Poe's "The Spectacles" (1844) and James's "Glasses" (1896) "has been overlooked" (187). Noting the similarity between the plots and themes of the works, Tintner asserts that Poe's tale served as James's source. While Tintner makes important observations about the stories, she does not explore fully a crucial connection between the two: the opera house as the location of the narrators' misperceptions and the heroines' deceptions.

5. "During the years Edith lived in New York with her parents, from 1872 to 1880, this enormous hotel was the center of the city's social, business, and political life. [. . .] At the outbreak of the Civil War the new hotel had become the headquarters of the forces organized to preserve the Union. Republican politicians made it their unofficial headquarters. The 'Amen Corner' of the lobby was where Platt, the Republican leader, would sit and give instructions to his minions. It was thronged with just the sort of people the Jones family loved to shun" (Dwight 22).

Works Cited

Abel, Samuel D. *Opera in the Flesh: Sexuality in Operatic Performance.* Boulder: Westview, 1996.

Ackerman, Alan Louis Jr. "Theatre and the Private Sphere in the Fiction of Louisa May Alcott." *Domestic Sphere: Reading the Nineteenth-Century Interior.* Ed. Inga Bryden and Janet Floyd. New York: Manchester University Press, 1999.

Agnew, Jean-Christophe. "The Consuming Vision of Henry James." *The Culture of Consumption: Critical Essays in American History, 1880–1980.* Ed. Richard Wrightman Fox and T. J. Jackson Lears. New York: Pantheon, 1983.

Alcott, Louisa May. *The Early Stories of Louisa May Alcott, 1852–1860.* New York: Ironweed Press, 2000.

The Authentic Librettos of the Wagner Operas. New York: Crown, 1938.

Bell, Millicent. *Edith Wharton and Henry James: The Story of Their Friendship.* London: Peter Owen, 1966.

Bellini, Vincenzo. *Norma: A Tragedy in Two Acts with Italian-English Text.* Melville: Belwin Mills Publishing Corp., 1980.

———. *La Sonnambula: An Opera in Two Acts with Italian and English Text.* New York: Edwin F. Kalmus, n.d.

Bisco, John. "Prospectus of the Broadway Journal." *Broadway Journal* 4 Jan. 1845: 16.

Bohlke, L. Brent, ed. *Willa Cather in Person: Interviews, Speeches, and Letters.* Lincoln: University of Nebraska Press, 1986.

Boren, Lynda. *Eurydice Reclaimed: Language, Gender, and Voice in Henry James.* Ann Arbor: UMI Research Press, 1989.

Broadway Journal. 22 Feb. 1845: 127.

Burwick, Frederick L. "Edgar Allan Poe: The Sublime and the Grotesque." *Prism(s): Essays in Romanticism* 8 (2000): 67–123.

Cather, Willa. *Collected Short Fiction: 1892–1912.* Ed. Virginia Faulkner. Lincoln: University of Nebraska Press, 1970.

———. "The Incomparable Opera House." *Nebraska History: A Quarterly Journal* 49.3 (1968): 373–78.

———. *The Kingdom of Art: Willa Cather's First Principles and Critical Statements, 1893–1896.* Ed. Bernice Slote. Lincoln: University of Nebraska Press, 1966.

———. *Not Under Forty.* New York: Alfred A. Knopf, 1900.
———. Preface. *The Wagnerian Romances.* By Gertrude Hall. New York: Alfred A. Knopf, 1925.
———. *The Song of the Lark.* Boston: Houghton Mifflin Company, 1937.
———. "Three American Singers." *McClure's Magazine* 42 (1913): 33–48.
———. *The World and the Parish.* Vol. 2. Lincoln: University of Nebraska Press, 1970.
———. *Youth and the Bright Medusa.* New York: Alfred A. Knopf, 1971.
Chodorow, Nancy. *The Reproduction of Mothering: Psychoanalysis and the Sociology of Gender.* Berkeley and Los Angeles: University of California Press, 1978.
Chopin, Kate. *The Awakening.* Ed. Margaret Culley. New York: W. W. Norton, 1976.
Chotia, Jean. *English Drama of the Early Modern Period, 1890–1940.* New York: Longman, 1996.
Christ, Carol P. *Diving Deep and Surfacing: Women Writers on Spiritual Quest.* Boston: Beacon, 1995.
Churchill, Allen. *The Upper Crust: An Informal History of New York's Highest Society.* New Jersey: Prentice-Hall, 1970.
Clayton, Ellen Creathorne. *Queens of Song: Being Memoirs of Some of the Most Celebrated Female Vocalists Who Have Performed on the Lyric Stage from the Earliest Days of Opera to the Present Time.* New York: Harper and Brothers, 1864.
"The Concert Room." *Broadway Journal* 22 June 1845: 124.
Cone, John Frederick. *First Rival of the Metropolitan Opera.* New York: Columbia University Press, 1983.
Cooke, Alice L. "Notes on Whitman's Musical Background." *New England Quarterly* 19 (1946): 224–35.
Cooke, Maud C. *Manual of Etiquette or Social Forms, Manners and Customs of Correct Society.* Cincinnati: Lyons Brothers and Co., 1896.
Corum, Carol S. "Music in *The Awakening.*" *Mount Olive Review* 8 (1995–96): 36–44.
"A Crowd at the Academy." Editorial. *New York Times* 23 Oct. 1883.
Davis, Peter G. *The American Opera Singer: The Lives and Adventures of America's Great Singers in Opera and Concert, from 1825 to the Present.* New York: Doubleday, 1997.
Dickstein, Morris. "The City as Text: New York and the American Writer." *TriQuarterly* 83 Winter (1991–92): 183–205.
Dizikes, John. *Opera in America: A Cultural History.* New Haven: Yale University Press, 1993.

Dwight, Eleanor. *Edith Wharton: An Extraordinary Life.* New York: Harry N. Abrams, 1994.

Dyson, J. Peter. "Romance and the Prima Donna Image in the Fiction of Henry James." *The Henry James Review* 12 (1991): 128–32.

Edel, Leon, and Lyall H. Powers, eds. *The Complete Notebooks of Henry James.* New York: Oxford University Press, 1987.

Eisler, Paul E. *The Metropolitan Opera: The First Twenty-Five Years, 1883–1908.* Croton-on-Hudson: North River Press, 1984.

Emerson, Ralph Waldo. *Essays: First and Second Series.* New York: Vintage, 1990.

Faner, Robert. *Walt Whitman and Opera.* Carbondale: Southern Illinois University Press, 1972.

Fisher, Benjamin F. "Poe and the Gothic Tradition." *The Cambridge Companion to Edgar Allan Poe.* Ed. Kevin J. Hayes. Cambridge: Cambridge University Press, 2002.

Foster, Shirley. "The Open Cage: Freedom, Marriage, and the Heroine in Early Twentieth-Century American Women's Novels." *Women's Writing: A Challenge to Theory.* Ed. Moira Monteith. New York: St. Martin's, 1986.

Foucault, Michel. *Discipline and Punish: The Birth of the Prison.* Trans. Alan Sheridan. New York: Pantheon, 1977.

"French Opera at the Park Theatre." *Broadway Journal* 28 June 1845: 410.

Furness, Joseph Clifton. *Walt Whitman's Workshop: A Collection of Unpublished Manuscripts.* New York: Russell and Russell, 1964.

Gallagher, Lowell. "Jenny Lind and the Voice of America." *En Travesti: Women, Gender Subversion, Opera.* Ed. Corrine E. Blackmer and Patricia Juliana Smith. New York: Columbia University Press, 1995.

Gargano, James W. "The Distorted Perception of Poe's Comic Narrators." *Topic: 30* 16 (1976): 23–34.

Giannone, Richard. *Music in Willa Cather's Fiction.* Lincoln: University of Nebraska Press, 1968.

Glicksberg, Charles I. *Walt Whitman and the Civil War: A Collection of Original Articles and Manuscripts.* Philadelphia: University of Pennsylvania Press, 1933.

Gluck, Christoph W. *Orfeo ed Euridice: A Lyric Play in Three Acts.* Libretto translated by Mandred Maggioni. New York: F. Rullman, n.d.

Gounod, Charles. *Faust: A Lyric Drama in Five Acts.* New York: Edwin F. Kalmus, 1972.

Gouverneur, Marian. *As I Remember: Recollections of American Society during the Nineteenth Century.* New York: D. Appleton and Co., 1911.

Greer, Germaine. *The Obstacle Race: The Fortunes of Women Painters and Their Work.* New York: Farrar, Straus, and Giroux, 1979.

Griffith, Kelley. "Wagnerian Romanticism in Kate Chopin's *The Awakening.*" *English Romanticism: Preludes and Postludes.* Ed. Donald Schoonmaker and John A. Alford. East Lansing: Colleagues Press, 1993.

Halliwell, Michael. *Opera and the Novel: The Case of Henry James.* New York: Rodopi, 2005.

Harbison, Sherrill. "Cather, Fremstad, and Wagner." *Willa Cather's New York: Essays on Cather in the City.* Ed. Merrill Maguire Skaggs. Madison: Fairleigh Dickinson University Press, 2000.

Harrison, James A., ed. *The Complete Works of Edgar Allan Poe.* 16 vols. New York: Fred de Fau and Co., 1902.

Hartley, Cecil B. *The Gentlemen's Book of Etiquette, and Manual of Politeness; Being A Complete Guide for a Gentleman's Conduct in All His Relations Towards Society.* Boston: J. S. Locke and Company, 1875.

Hartley, Florence. *The Ladies' Book of Etiquette, and Manual of Politeness: A Complete Handbook for the Use of the Lady in Polite Society.* Boston: J. S. Locke and Company, 1875.

Hodges, Laura F. "Recognizing "False Notes': Musical Rhetoric in *The Portrait of a Lady.*" *Mosaic: A Journal for the Interdisciplinary Study of Literature* 32 (1999): 1–16.

Holloway, Emory. "Whitman as His Own Press-Agent." *American Mercury* 18 (1929): 482–88.

Homberger, Eric. *Mrs. Astor's New York: Money and Social Power in a Gilded Age.* New Haven: Yale University Press, 2002.

"Home News." *Broadway Journal* 8 March 1845: 158.

Homans, Margaret. *Bearing the Word: Language and Female Experience in Nineteenth-Century Women's Writing.* Chicago: University of Chicago Press, 1986.

Horne, Philip, ed. *Henry James: A Life in Letters.* New York: Viking, 1999.

Horner, Avril, and Sue Zlosnik. *Gothic and the Comic Turn.* New York: Palgrave Macmillan, 2005.

Horowitz, Joseph. *Wagner Nights: An American History.* Berkeley and Los Angeles: University of California Press, 1994.

Huf, Linda. *A Portrait of the Artist as a Young Woman: The Writer as Heroine in American Literature.* New York: Frederick Ungar, 1983.

Hutcheon, Linda, and Michael Hutcheon. *Bodily Charm: Living Opera.* Lincoln: University of Nebraska Press, 2000.

Irwin, John T. "Self-Evidence and Self-Reference: Nietzsche and Tragedy, Whitman and Opera." *New Literary History* 11 (1979): 177–92.

Ivry, Benjamin. "Portrait of an Author." *Opera News* 53 (1988): 20–21.

Jaher, Frederic Cople. "Style and Status: High Society in Late Nineteenth-Century New York." *The Rich, the Well Born, and the Powerful: Elites and Upper Classes in History.* Ed. Frederic Cople Jaher. Urbana: University of Illinois Press, 1973.

James, Henry. *The American.* New York: W. W. Norton, 1978.

———. *The American Scene.* New York: St. Martin's, 1987.

———. *The Complete Tales of Henry James.* 12 vols. Ed. Leon Edel. New York: J. B. Lippincott, 1962.

———. *Embarrassments.* New York: Macmillan, 1897.

———. *Essays in London and Elsewhere.* New York: Harper and Brothers, 1893.

———. *Henry James Letters.* Ed. Leon Edel. Vol. 2: 1875–1883. Cambridge: Belknap Press of Harvard University Press, 1975.

———. *Parisian Sketches: Letters to the New York Tribune 1875–1876.* New York: New York University Press, 1957.

———. *The Portrait of a Lady.* Ed. Robert D. Bamberg. New York: W. W. Norton, 1995.

———. *A Small Boy and Others.* New York: Charles Scribner's Sons, 1913.

Johnson, Patricia E. "The Gendered Politics of the Gaze: Henry James and George Eliot." *Mosaic: A Journal of the Interdisciplinary Study of Literature* 30.1 (1997): 39–54.

Kerman, Joseph. *Opera as Drama.* New York: Alfred A. Knopf, 1956.

Ketterer, David. *The Rationale of Deception in Poe.* Baton Rouge: Louisiana State University Press, 1979.

Kmen, Henry A. *Music in New Orleans: The Formative Years, 1791–1841.* Baton Rouge: Louisiana State University Press, 1966.

Koestenbaum, Wayne. *The Queen's Throat: Opera, Homosexuality, and the Mystery of Desire.* New York: Poseidon, 1993.

Korsmeyer, Carolyn. "Perceptions, Pleasures, Arts: Considering Aesthetics." *Philosophy in a Feminist Voice: Critiques and Reconstructions.* Ed. Janet A. Kourany. Princeton: Princeton University Press, 1998.

Kramer, Lawrence. *After the Lovedeath: Sexual Violence and the Making of a Culture.* Berkeley and Los Angeles: University of California Press, 1997.

———. *Music as a Cultural Practice, 1800–1900.* Berkeley and Los Angeles: University of California Press, 1990.

Krause, Sydney J. "Whitman, Music, and Proud Music of the Storm." *PMLA* 72 (1957): 705–21.

Krehbiel, Henry Edward. *Chapters of Opera: Historical and Critical Observations and Records Concerning the Lyric Drama in New York from Its Earliest Days Down to the Present Time.* New York: Henry Holt and Co., 1908.

Lacan, Jacques. *Écrits: A Selection.* Trans. Alan Sheridan. New York: W. W. Norton, 1977.

Lemco, Gary. "Henry James and Richard Wagner: *The American.*" *Hartford Studies in Literature* 6 (1974): 147–58.

Leonardi, Susan J. "To Have a Voice: The Politics of the Diva." *Perspectives on Contemporary Literature* 13 (1987): 65–72.

Leonardi, Susan J., and Rebecca A. Pope. *The Diva's Mouth; Body, Voice, and Prima Donna Politics.* New Brunswick: Rutgers University Press, 1996.

Lewis, Edith. *Willa Cather Living.* Athens: Ohio University Press, 1989.

Lindenberger, Herbert. *Opera: The Extravagant Art.* Ithaca: Cornell University Press, 1984.

———. *Opera in History: From Monteverdi to Cage.* Stanford: Stanford University Press, 1998.

Luria, Sarah. "The Architecture of Manners: Henry James, Edith Wharton, and the Mount." *American Quarterly* 49 (1997): 298–327.

McClary, Susan. *Feminine Endings: Music, Gender, and Sexuality.* Minneapolis: University of Minnesota Press, 1991.

McConachie, Bruce A. "New York Operagoing, 1825–50: Creating an Elite Social Ritual." *American Music* 6 (1988): 181–92.

Merlin, Countess de. *Memoirs and Letters of Madame Malibran.* Vol. 1. Philadelphia: Carey and Hart, 1840.

Montgomery, Maureen E. *Displaying Women: Spectacles of Leisure in Edith Wharton's New York.* New York: Routledge, 1998.

Morris, Lloyd. *Incredible New York: High Life and Low Life of the Last Hundred Years.* New York: Random House, 1951.

Mulvey, Laura. "Visual Pleasures and Narrative Cinema." *Visual and Other Pleasures.* Bloomington: Indiana University Press, 1989.

Mumford, Lewis. *The Brown Decades: A Study of the Arts in America, 1865–1895.* New York: Dover, 1955.

"Musical Items." *Broadway Journal* 22 March 1845: 190.

Myerson, Joel, Daniel Shealy, and Madeleine B. Stern, eds. *The Journals of Louisa May Alcott.* Boston: Little, Brown, 1989.

Nochlin, Linda. *Women, Art, and Power and Other Essays.* New York: Harper and Row, 1988.

O'Brien, Sharon. *Willa Cather: The Emerging Voice.* New York: Oxford University Press, 1987.

"The Opera." *The New-York Literary Gazette, and Phi Beta Kappa Repository* 17 Dec. 1825: 239.

"Operas and Concerts." *Broadway Journal* 25 Jan. 1845: 59.

Poizat, Michel. *The Angel's Cry: Beyond the Pleasure Principle in Opera*. Ithaca: Cornell University Press, 1992.

Pound, Louise. "Walt Whitman and Italian Music." *American Mercury* 6 (1925): 58–63.

Powers, Lyall H., ed. *Henry James and Edith Wharton, Letters: 1900–1915*. New York: Charles Scribner's Sons, 1990.

Reichardt, Ulfried. "Interior and Exterior Spaces: Versions of the Self in the American Novel around 1900." *Space in America: Theory, History, Culture*. Ed. Klaus Benesch and Kerstin Schmidt. New York: Rodopi, 2005.

Ringe, Donald, A. *American Gothic: Imagination and Reason in Nineteenth-Century Fiction*. Lexington: University Press of Kentucky, 1982.

Rosowski, Susan. "The Novel of Awakening." *Genre* 12 (1979): 313–32.

Saunders, Judith P. "'If This I Saw': Optic Dilemmas in Poe's Writings." *American Transcendental Quarterly* 62 (1986): 63–80.

Sergeant, Elizabeth Shepley. *Willa Cather: A Memoir*. Lincoln: University of Nebraska Press, 1963.

Sessa, Anne Dzamba. *Richard Wagner and the English*. London: Associated University Presses, 1979.

Seyersted, Per. *Kate Chopin: A Critical Biography*. Baton Rouge: Louisiana State University Press, 1969.

Silverman, Kenneth. *Edgar Allan Poe: Mournful and Never-Ending Remembrance*. New York: Harper Collins Publishers, 1991.

Skaggs, Merrill M. "Key Modulations in Cather's Novels about Music." *Willa Cather Pioneer Memorial Newsletter* 39.2–3 (1995): 25–30.

Solie, Ruth A. "Fictions of the Opera Box." *The Work of Opera: Genre, Nationhood, and Sexual Difference*. Ed. Richard Dellamora and Daniel Fischlin. New York: Columbia University Press, 1997.

Spiegelman, Julia. "Walt Whitman and Music." *South Atlantic Quarterly* 41 (1942): 167–76.

Stern, Madeleine B. "Louisa Alcott, Trouper: Experiences in Theatricals, 1848–1880." *New England Quarterly* 16 (1943): 175–97.

Stout, Janis. *A Calendar of the Letters of Willa Cather*. Lincoln: University of Nebraska Press, 2002.

———. *Willa Cather: The Writer and Her World*. Charlottesville: University Press of Virginia, 2000.

Tintner, Adeline R. *The Book World of Henry James: Appropriating the Classics*. Ann Arbor: UMI Research Press, 1987.

———. *The Cosmopolitan World of Henry James: An Intertextual Study*. Baton Rouge: Louisiana State University Press, 1991.

———. "Jamesian Structures in *The Age of Innocence* and Related Stories." *Twentieth Century Literature* 26 (1980): 332–47.

Toth, Emily. "Kate Chopin's Music." *Regionalism and the Female Imagination* 3 (1977): 27–29.

Toth, Emily, and Per Seyersted, eds. *Kate Chopin's Private Papers.* Bloomington: Indiana University Press, 1998.

Traubel, Horace, ed. *With Walt Whitman in Camden.* 3 vols. New York: Rowman and Littlefield, 1961.

Trowbridge, John Townsend. "Reminiscences of Walt Whitman." *Atlantic Monthly* 89 (1902): 163–75.

Tuttleton, James W. *The Novel of Manners in America.* Chapel Hill: University of North Carolina Press, 1972.

Veblen, Thorstein. *The Theory of the Leisure Class.* New Brunswick: Transaction, 1992.

Wagner, Richard. *Prelude and Transfiguration from Tristan and Isolde.* Ed. Robert Bailey. New York: W. W. Norton, 1985.

———. *Opera and Drama.* Vol. 2 of *Richard Wagner's Prose Works.* Trans. William Ashton Ellis. New York: Broude Brothers, 1966.

———. *Religion and Art.* Vol. 4 of *Richard Wagner's Prose Works.* Trans. William Ashton Ellis. New York: Broude Brothers, 1966.

———. *Tristan and Isolde.* Libretto trans. by Andrew Porter. New York: Riverrun, 1981.

Weatherford, K. J. "Courageous Souls: Kate Chopin's Women Artists." *American Studies in Scandinavia.* 26 (1994): 96–112.

Wharton, Edith. *A Backward Glance.* New York: Charles Scribner's Sons, 1964.

———. *The Custom of the Country.* New York: Charles Scribner's Sons, 1941.

———. *The House of Mirth.* Ed. Elizabeth Ammons. New York: W. W. Norton, 1990.

———. *The Letters of Edith Wharton.* Ed. R. W. B. Lewis and Nancy Lewis. New York: Charles Scribner's Sons, 1988.

———. *Old New York.* New York: Charles Scribner's Sons, 1924.

———. *The Uncollected Critical Writings.* Ed. Frederick Wegener. Princeton: Princeton University Press, 1996.

Whitman, Walt. *The Complete Writings of Walt Whitman.* 10 vols. New York: G. P. Putnam's Sons, 1902.

———. *The Gathering of the Forces.* Ed. Cleveland Rodgers and John Black. 2 vols. New York: G. P. Putnam's Sons, 1920.

———. *Leaves of Grass.* Comprehensive Reader's Edition. Ed. Harold W. Blodgett and Sculley Bradley. New York: New York University Press, 1965.

———. *New York Dissected.* Ed. Emory Holloway and Ralph Adimari. New York: Rufus Rockwell Wilson, 1936.

———. *The Uncollected Poetry and Prose of Walt Whitman.* Ed. Emory Holloway. 2 vols. Gloucester: Peter Smith, 1972.

Williams, Anne. *Art of Darkness: A Poetics of Gothic.* Chicago: University of Chicago Press, 1995.

Wordsworth, William. *William Wordsworth: The Major Works.* Ed. Stephen Gill. Oxford: Oxford University Press, 2000.

Index